W9-BYA-777

media

MANUAL

Single-Camera Video Production

Fourth Edition

media
MANUAL

Series editor: Peter Ward

Single-Camera Video Production

Fourth Edition

Robert B. Musburger

AMSTERDAM • BOSTON • HEIDELBERG • LONDON • NEW YORK • OXFORD
PARIS • SAN DIEGO • SAN FRANCISCO • SINGAPORE • SYDNEY • TOKYO
Focal Press is an imprint of Elsevier

Acquisitions Editor: Elinor Actipis
Associate Acquisitions Editor: Christine Tridente
Project Manager: Anne B. McGee
Assistant Editor: Cara Anderson
Marketing Manager: Christine Degon

Focal Press is an imprint of Elsevier
30 Corporate Drive, Suite 400, Burlington, MA 01803, USA
Linacre House, Jordan Hill, Oxford OX2 8DP, UK

∞ Recognizing the importance of preserving what has been written, Elsevier prints its books on acid-free paper whenever possible.

Library of Congress Cataloging-in-Publication Data
Application submitted.

British Library Cataloguing-in-Publication Data
A catalogue record for this book is available from the British Library.

ISBN: 0-240-80706-5

For information on all Focal Press publications
visit our website at www.books.elsevier.com

05 06 07 08 09 10 10 9 8 7 6 5 4 3 2 1

Printed in the United States of America

Working together to grow libraries in developing countries

www.elsevier.com | www.bookaid.org | www.sabre.org

ELSEVIER   BOOK AID International   Sabre Foundation

*To my mother, Mary Tomazina Wemple Musburger Houska,
for teaching me the value of integrating art and technology.*

Contents

THE PRODUCTION PROCESS: PREPRODUCTION

THE PRODUCTION PROCESS: PRODUCTION

THE PRODUCTION PROCESS: POSTPRODUCTION

Introduction

This text has been written to provide three groups of video enthusiasts with enough information to produce acceptable single-camera video productions: the media production student, the professional who needs a refresher in the basics, and the first-time video camera owner. It is a basic, introductory book designed to point the beginner in the right direction.

This is not an advanced book in preproduction research and writing, nor is it a book on advanced techniques in electronic editing. Each of those subjects deserves its own title.

I wrote this book from three points of view: first, from that of an instructor introducing the techniques that lead to quality video productions using a single video camera; second, from that of a practitioner who has spent 50 years working in professional television and learning the contents of this book the hard way—that is, by making mistakes until I finally got it right; and third, from that of an academic fielding 20 phone calls per week from people new to electronic production who desperately want information about single-camera video production.

This book outlines the process of working with a single video camera from beginning to end, with an emphasis on the actual production process. First, however, you must lay some groundwork before picking up your camera. The video camera and recorder remain two complex pieces of equipment, despite efforts to simplify them. The process by which a video image is created is also complex, and you must understand it to properly utilize the benefits and master the restrictions of the medium.

The first section of this book contains a simplified explanation of how and why the video and audio signals are created. It also describes the technical restrictions in a video system. The second section describes the equipment: cameras; recorders; and audio, lighting, and mounting equipment. With the first two sections providing a firm base, the third and fourth sections carry you through the production process from preproduction planning (which is much more important than most beginners realize) to setting up, rehearsing, shooting, and striking. The final section touches on the postproduction process and the importance of shooting for the editing process.

As the media production world rapidly moves toward a nearly all-digital environment, I have included those changes that are critical for single-camera production. From experience, I am aware that the rapid changes will necessitate new information on virtually a monthly basis. I have attempted to anticipate some of those changes, but at the same time I have avoided making any wild guesses as to the next level of production changes. There are too many new concepts and proposals in process; some of them will be working years from now, others will be gone within 6 months. All we can do is watch and take advantage of what the field has to offer. Also, keep in mind that it is not the paintbrush that makes the difference, it is in the mind and from the hands of the artist.

Additional Comments on the Fourth Edition

The greatest technical change since the publication of the previous edition of this book is in the miniaturization of equipment and the movement away from all moving parts and to solid-state options. A key factor in the move of media toward an "all-digital" production format is the realization that all media must start in an analog format and, for humans to comprehend the messages, they must be returned to an analog format. Media converted to a digital format may be easily manipulated without loss of quality, but it cannot be viewed or listened to until converted into a form that the human eye and ear can interpret. For that reason, analog theory and technology remain a critical part of this book and will continue to be until humans can directly interpret a digital signal.

Acknowledgments

One cannot work in the video business without relying on many other people. This is not a solitary business, and throughout the years many people have made major contributions to my knowledge and my career, specifically Parks Whitmer and Sam Scott, who gave me my start in media production and kept me going; Art Mosby, who signed my first television paycheck; Bob Wormington, who let me develop my directing skills; the thousands of students at Avila College, University of Missouri at Kansas City, Kansas University, Florida State University, and the University of Houston, who constantly reminded me that I don't know everything there is to know about media production; and my wife, Pat, who lets me think that I do.

Thanks to Mark Mulvey for many new illustrations in this edition. Thanks also to all of the helpful people at Focal Press who have guided and prodded me through my publishing efforts: Karen, Philip, Mary, Trish, Marie, Maura, Tammy, Tricia, Lilly, Jennifer, Amy, and, for this edition, Elinor, Cara, Christine, and Suzanne.

The Technology

The Importance of Technology

If a would-be artist were to suddenly pick up a brush and start to dab paint on a canvas, or any other handy surface, the chances of achieving an immediate masterpiece would be minimal. The same holds true for a sculptor. One does not attack a piece of marble with a chisel without first learning the skills necessary to properly mold the form without damaging the original material or exceeding the capabilities of the medium.

Likewise, running through the woods with an out-of-focus camera may seem creative, but it is neither good art nor good video. An understanding of the basic technology of any art form is necessary to use properly the artistic characteristics of that medium and to avoid the pitfalls of its technical limitations.

Video is highly technical; the medium requires some basic knowledge of optics, electronics, electricity, physics, and mathematics. Of course, a video production can be completed without any knowledge of these subjects, but the possibility of it being a high-quality production is limited.

With the development of lighter, smaller, and more powerful equipment that operates using digital technology, you can create higher-quality video productions at a lower cost than was possible a few years ago. However, the advances in digital technology that make for better productions also require some knowledge of the digital domain and how it can and should be used in video production. Such digital equipment operates easily and with minimum knowledge of the media production process, but the ease of operation does not replace the thinking and creativity that is necessary for a quality production.

To use video cameras and associated audio equipment effectively, you must be aware of the capabilities and limitations of each piece of equipment. In addition, you must know how each piece of equipment operates in relation to other equipment used in the same production. This awareness does not necessarily mean having a broad range of knowledge of the technology involved in media production but rather having an appreciation and understanding of why the equipment is designed to operate as it does and what it can accomplish. Most important, it is necessary to understand what it *cannot* be expected to accomplish. Digital equipment does not replace the knowledge of composition, shot sequencing, or the construction of characters and story lines necessary to assemble a professional production. In fact, the basics of production are even more important in digital production because of the high level of resolution and clarity made possible in the digital formats. This clarity reveals poor lighting, bad framing, incorrect exposure, and all other gaffes that would barely manifest in analog production.

2

PLANNED ART
VS. UNPLANNED ART

Art by Accident

Art by Plan

Limitations of Equipment

The human eye and ear are two extraordinary instruments for sensing light and sound. No human invention has ever come close to matching the capabilities of those two sensory organs. It is easy to forget how limited the electronic aural and visual equipment are until we compare them to their human counterparts.

The human eye can focus from nearly the end of the nose to infinity instantaneously. The eye can adjust to light variations quickly and can pick out images in light varying more than 1,000 times from the lightest to the darkest. The human ear can hear sounds varying in loudness from 0 decibels to more than 160 decibels and can respond to frequency changes from 15 hertz to more than 20,000 hertz.

The best professional digital camera cannot reveal detail in light variations greater than 80:1; most prosumer cameras have difficulty creating acceptable images beyond a contrast range of 40:1. The best lenses have limited focus range, and the depth of field depends on the amount of light present and focal length and f-stop settings. The best microphone is limited to less than 60 decibels in loudness range. Most audio equipment cannot reproduce frequencies beyond a range of 10,000 hertz without inconsistent variations. Digital equipment allows repeated duplication of signals without degradation, but it does little to extend the dynamic range of either sound or video.

It is important to remember that the audio/video equipment converts sound and light to electronic impulses and that, regardless of the expense or quality of the equipment used, it cannot capture everything that the human eye and ear can capture. The newest developments in digital cameras and audio processing have extended the ability of the recording process to more closely reproduce what a human can see and hear. However, the limitations of the equipment, whether analog or digital, taped or recorded on solid state, still play a crucial role in the planning of a video production.

SUPERIORITY OF HUMAN SENSES

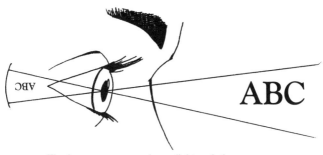

The human eye reproduces light variations
at a ratio of more than 1000:1.

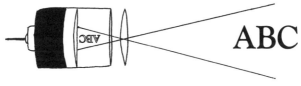

The best video camera can reproduce
light variations only at a 30:1 ratio.

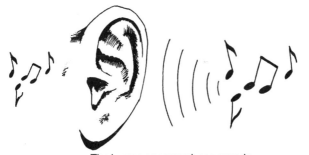

The human ear reproduces sounds
as loud as 160 decibels.

The best microphones reproduce sounds
no louder than 60 decibels.

Limitations of Equipment

5

The Audio Signal: Frequency

The audio signal has two basic characteristics: frequency (tone) and amplitude (loudness). To create with and record sound, these two characteristics must be understood. All sounds start as an analog signal because the vibration in air that creates sound is an analog motion. Digital sound is created within the equipment and must be converted back to analog for humans to hear it.

Frequency is measured in *hertz* (or cycles per second), usually abbreviated as Hz. Because most of the sounds humans can hear are more than 1,000 Hz, the abbreviation kHz (representing kilohertz) often is used; k is the abbreviation for *kilo-,* the metric equivalent of 1,000.

A *cycle* is the time or distance between peaks of a single sound vibration. A single continuous frequency is called a *tone* and is often used for testing. Humans perceive frequency as *pitch,* the highness and lowness of tones. The term *timbre* is a musical term often used in media production that refers to the special feeling a sound may have as a result of its source. For example, a note struck on the piano may be the same frequency as that of the same note played on a trumpet, but the timbre is very different.

The energy spectrum ranges from 0 Hz to greater than a *yottahertz*—a septillion hertz (a billion, billion, million hertz). The frequency range most humans can hear is between 10 Hz and 20 kHz. Frequencies greater than the audible human range include *radiofrequencies* (RFs) used as broadcast carrier waves, microwaves, X-rays and light, or the visible spectrum.

Most analog videotape recorders can record only audio frequencies between 30 Hz and 10 kHz. Digital recorders are capable of recording a broader range, but because human hearing is limited, so is digital recording. The frequencies excluded in recordings are not generally missed unless the production requires a wide range of frequency response, such as a music session.

The range of frequency response and certain portions of frequencies may be modified as needed for an individual production. This altering of the frequency response is called *equalization.* When you adjust the tone controls, treble or bass, on a stereo, you are equalizing the signal by modifying the frequency response. Although most videotape recorders do not have equalization controls, some audio mixers and microphones do.

THE FREQUENCY SPECTRUM

Frequency	Frequency Uses	Type of Wave
0-10kH	Audio	Sound
10kH-100kH	Experimental, Maritime Navigation & Comm.	Very Low Freq.
100kH-1MH	Maritime & Aviation Navigation & Comm. & Ham	Low Freq.
1 MH-10MH	AM B-cast, Ham, Radio Navigation, Industrial	Medium Freq.
10MH-100MH	Int'l Shortwave, Ham, Citizens, Medical, LORAN	High Freq.
100MH-1GH	Aviation, TV B-cast, FM B-cast, FAX, Ham, Wx	Very High Freq.
1GH-10GH	Aviation, STL Microwave, Gov., TV B-cast, Ham	Ultra High Freq.
10GH-100GH	Gov., Radio Nav., Ham, Fixed & Mobile	Super High Freq.
100GH-1TH	Experimental, Government, Ham	Extremely Hi.Freq
1TH-10TH	Industrial Photo, Research	Infrared
10TH-100TH	Heat Waves	Infrared
100TH-1PH	Heat Waves	Infrared
1PH-10PH	Light-Heat Waves	Light-Ultraviolet
10PH-100PH	Ionizing Radiation, Medical Research	Ultraviolet
100PH-1EH	Ionizing Radiation, Medical Research	Soft X-rays
1EH-10EH	Ionizing Radiation, Scientific Research	X-rays
10EH-100EH	Gamma Rays	Hard X-rays
100EH-1 ZH	Gamma Rays	Hard X-rays

The Higher Metric Classifications

KILO	1,000	Thousand
MEGA	1,000,000	Million
GIGA	1,000,000,000	Billion
TERA	1,000,000,000,000	Trillion
PETA	1,000,000,000,000,000	Quadrillion
EXA	1,000,000,000,000,000,000	Quintillion
ZETTA	1,000,000,000,000,000,000,000	Sextillion
YOTTA	1,000,000,000,000,000,000,000,000	Septillion

Frequency Spectrum Chart

The Audio Signal: Amplitude

Amplitude is the energy level of the audio signal. The listener perceives amplitude as loudness. Relative amplitude is referred to as level and is measured in *decibels,* abbreviated as dB. *Deci-* is one tenth on the metric scale, and *bel* is the measure of audio amplitude created by Alexander Graham Bell. Because the bel is a very large unit of measure, dB is more commonly used. The decibel is a somewhat confusing unit of measurement because it is a reference measurement of the change of the power of the signal. It is not an absolute measurement, and it is logarithmic, not linear; it can be expressed in either volts or watts. A change of at least 3 dB is necessary for the human ear to perceive a change in level. Levels are measured in both positive and negative decibels.

Volume is the term used when referring to the measurable energy that translates into loudness and that may be measured in either volume units (VUs) or decibels. Humans are sensitive to a change in volume, but human hearing is not linear. At some frequencies and at some volume levels, the ear senses a change but the actual measure of change is not registered accurately within the human brain. Robinson–Dadson Loudness Curves indicate the relative sensitivity humans have to various frequencies and loudness levels. Because analog audio equipment can handle a volume change no greater than approximately 60 dB, and even though digital recording equipment can handle a greater dynamic range, accurate level readings must be available during recording to avoid distorted or noisy sound in either analog or digital systems. There are two aberrations of audio to watch for: distortion and noise. *Distortion* is an unwanted change in the audio signal. The most common distortion is caused by attempting to record the audio at a level too high for the equipment. In digital audio systems, high levels may cause the audio to skip or cease entirely. Analog-distorted sounds are warped, wavering, or massive variations from the original sound. *Noise* is unwanted sound added to the audio. Digital systems are very sensitive to all sounds; therefore, noise may be added to a recording if not adequately monitored. Analog noise may be introduced into a program if the audio level is too low. If the level is too low, tape hiss or other sounds generated within the system may be heard and added to the original sound.

AMPLITUDE VERSUS FREQUENCY

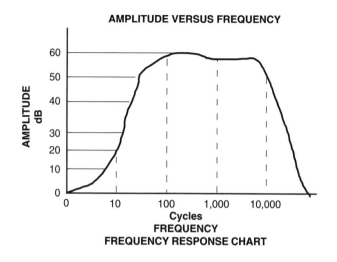

FREQUENCY RESPONSE CHART

ROBINSON-DADSON LOUDNESS CURVES

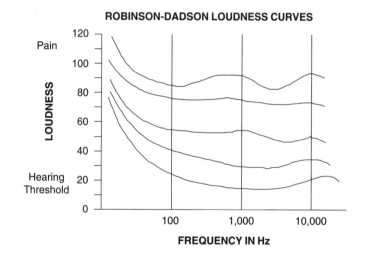

Measuring Audio

The audio level can be measured as it is being recorded using a VU meter, a peak-to-peak meter, or light-emitting diodes (LEDs). Each of these gives the operator an indication of the level of the audio. When the level is too high, the meters read greater than the 0 dB indicator; with LEDs, the changing color of the flashing diodes indicates the audio level. When the level is too low, the meter needles barely move, and few, if any, diodes flash.

The audio operator attempts to keep dynamic levels within the specified range of equipment, whether digital or analog, by attenuating the level (decreasing it) when the audio source is too loud and boosting the level (increasing it) when the audio source level is too low. This is called *riding gain,* and it may be done either manually by the operator or automatically by circuits built into the equipment called *automatic gain controls* (AGCs) or *automatic level controls* (ALCs). AGCs and ALCs will maintain certain maximum and minimum levels, but they may add noise by boosting levels during a soft or quiet passage or by overdriving if there is a sudden, loud increase in the input.

Dynamics refers to the difference between the loudest and the quietest passage. Most analog equipment is limited to a range of approximately 60 dB; newer digital equipment features dynamic ranges greater than 100 dB. Crickets at night might be heard at 3 dB, a normal conversation at 100 dB, and a rock concert at 130 dB or greater (which is above the threshold of pain and can be damaging to hearing).

To achieve the greatest possible audio quality, record and reproduce sound as close to the original as possible. Even though it is not possible to record all frequencies at the exact same level as the original sound was recorded, a successful operator makes the effort to exclude all noise and to avoid distorting the audio signal.

Two additional measurements are required for digital audio: *sampling* and *quantization.* Sampling is the number of times per second analog sound is measured as it is converted to digital. To transfer the maximum quality, samplings need to be done at twice the greatest expected frequency to be converted. Currently, the standard sampling rate is 48 kHz. Compact discs are sampled at 44.1 kHz. *Quantization* is the number of discrete levels at which analog sound is measured as it is converted. The greater the bit rate of quantization, the higher the quality of the conversion. Currently, 32- to 64-bit quantization is considered the professional rate. Increasing both the sampling and quantization rates increases the demand for memory and bandwidth for digital moving files.

CYCLE AND LOUDNESS CURVES
One Complete Cycle

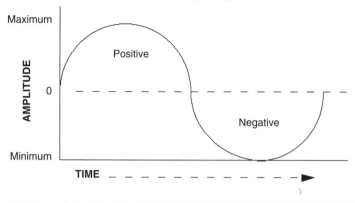

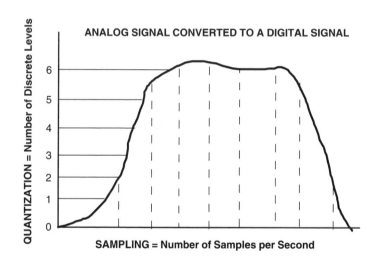

The Video Signal

The video signal, like the audio signal, is made up of voltages varying in frequency and level. Even though the video electronic signal is complex, it should be considered in much the same manner as the audio signal. The camera cannot record all that the eye can see, nor can a videotape recorder—whether analog or digital—process all the information fed into it. Avoid video distortion and noise as vehemently as you avoid audio distortion and noise.

Video distortion and noise are defined in much the same way as audio distortion and noise, except that you can see video distortion as flare in brightly lit areas, as tearing, or as color shifts in the picture; video noise can be seen as a grainy or "crawly" texture to the picture.

Changing Light into Electrons

The process of changing light into electrons is a transducing process involving two major changes in energy. The first change is the collection and concentration of light reflected from the subject onto the surface of the instrument that changes the light to electrons. The second change in energy is the transformation of that light to an electronic signal. Following are the three primary functions of a video camera lens:

- To collect as much light reflected from the subject as possible
- To control how much light passes through the lens
- To focus the image on the photosensitive surface of the camera

The secondary function of a video camera lens is to provide a certain field of view, either with a fixed-focal-length (prime) lens or with a variable-focal-length (zoom) lens. The *field of view* is the area the camera can see in any one shot.

Light concentrated by the lens onto the surface of the transducer is transformed into electronics by solid-state image sensors called *chips.* Chips are a light-sensitive, solid-state device known as a metal oxide semiconductor (MOS chip, or a charge-coupled device [CCD]). The chips vary in size from $1/3$ to $3/4$ square inch and less than $1/8$ inch in thickness. Digital Cinema (DC) cameras may use chips as large as 35 mm ($\sim$1.5 inches). As the light strikes the surfaces of the chips, an electronic scan beam is altered in proportion to the intensity of the light falling on that specific part of the light-sensitive surface. The brighter the light, the greater the reaction, whereas the lower the light, the smaller the reaction.

Although light is an analog system, once the signal leaves the transducer, it can be converted to an analog or a digital electronic signal.

12

CHANGING LIGHT INTO ELECTRONS

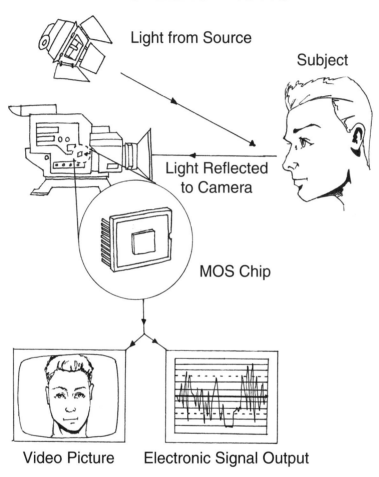

Light from Source

Subject

Light Reflected to Camera

MOS Chip

Video Picture Electronic Signal Output

The Scanning System

To reproduce the changes in light converted to electronics, a system was devised to create a changing light in the television receiver or monitor that matched that of the camera. This was accomplished through the use of a scanning system in the receiver that matched the one in the camera. A beam of electrons starts scanning the chip and the receiver at the same time. Completely scanning the frame, called a raster, in the National Television Standards Committee (NTSC) system requires 525 lines, 262.5 at a time, in a pattern called a field. The second 262.5 lines scanned are slightly offset from the first set in a pattern called interlaced scanning. The total scanning of the two 262.5-line fields is one 525-line frame that occurs once every $\frac{1}{30}$ of a second. The line-scanning system must match that of the receiver and operate in the same manner so that the picture can be duplicated exactly as originally shot in the camera. Knowledge about the scanning system is not crucial to video production, except that the camera operator must be aware that the reproduction system is not based on complete coverage of the field. Instead, the reproduction system is based on a series of 525 horizontal lines (or more) that make reproducing fine horizontal lines in a picture difficult. The scan system also limits the vertical resolution power of the video system.

Proposals for revising the scanning system, the aspect ratio, the number of lines, and a progressive scan system rather than the current NTSC interlace scan system are in effect in the United States. The U.S. Federal Communications Commission (FCC) has released a set of standards for digital broadcasting in this country. Currently, there are actually 18 different digital television standards. The line rate varies from 360 to 1,080. The scan system may be NTSC interlace—that is, two fields making up one frame—or a progressive scan that scans the entire frame from top to bottom. The frame rate may vary from 24 to 60 frames per second (fps). In between, one can find 30, 29.97, 50, and 59.94 fps. The 59.94 and 29.97 rates came about after 1953, when the NTSC signal was modified to carry color signals. The slight difference is called drop-frame and is important only in productions longer than a few minutes. The aspect ratio may be 4:3 (NTSC or Phase Alternating Line [PAL; British System]) or 16:9 (wide-screen). The wide variety of systems and combinations may someday be reduced, but for the time being, each person involved in the production process needs to be aware of which system the producer expects to use to release the production. The signals can be converted, but the highest quality and fewest problems come from agreeing on the standard before the first frame is shot (see "Digital Signal Standards").

SCAN SYSTEMS

NTSC INTERLACE
Two field, one frame

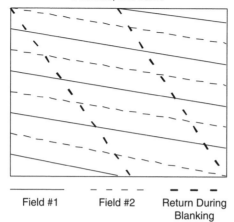

| Field #1 | Field #2 | Return During Blanking |

PROGRESSIVE
One field, one frame

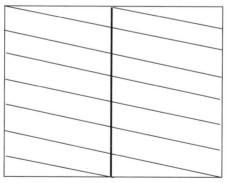

| Continuous Scan | Return During Blanking |

The Synchronization Process

To reproduce the picture on the home receiver exactly as it was shot in the camera, the signal must contain a component that keeps the lines and frames in synchronization. The scan line in the receiver must start at precisely the same time as the picture is being scanned in the camera, and a new frame must start exactly at the same time as the new frame is started in the camera. This timing sequence is critical, and it involves small fractions of time. Each NTSC frame lasts $\frac{1}{30}$ of a second, each field lasts $\frac{1}{60}$ of a second, and a new line starts every $\frac{1}{15,700}$ of a second in the 525-line system. In the many other scan and line rate systems, the rates are different, but all must match the receiver. A PAL receiver or tape deck will not synchronize with an NTSC signal and vice versa; the two systems are not compatible. One of the goals of developing an international high-definition television (HDTV) standard was to create a standard that all countries would follow, but this has not happened, partially because of different power line rates in each country. U.S. power is a 60-cycle system, whereas much of the rest of the world uses a variation of a 50-cycle system.

For this complex system to stay in synchronization, pulses are added between the fields and between the lines. These are called sync pulses, and they must be created either in the camera or in a sync generator. The sync pulses are part of the recorded signal, and the receiver or tape deck locks onto those pulses when the tape is played back or the signal is broadcast. The pulses can be corrected if there are errors in their timing by running the signal through a time base corrector (TBC). A TBC can correct some sync errors and some variations in picture quality, but it cannot correct all errors.

ELECTRONIC SIGNAL OF TWO FIELDS AS SEEN ON THE FACE OF A WAVEFORM MONITOR (OSCILLOSCOPE)

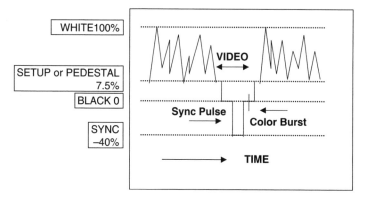

WHITE100%

SETUP or PEDESTAL 7.5%

BLACK 0

SYNC −40%

VIDEO

Sync Pulse

Color Burst

TIME

Color Video

Previous discussion in this chapter has focused on the black-and-white, or luminance, characteristic of the video signal. To create and reproduce a color signal, the other characteristic of light, the chrominance, or color portion, must be addressed. The 525-line system was agreed on early in the history of the development of television in the United States by the NTSC. In 1941 (just before World War II), equipment that could be manufactured at a reasonable cost could accommodate no more than 525 lines. That standard has been altered as digital HDTV, a higher resolution system using more lines and a wider scan ratio, has been developed (see "Digital Signal Standards").

After World War II, the NTSC decided that the best method of adding color to black-and-white televisions was to use an all-electronic system and recommended adoption of the RCA-compatible system.

The RCA system separated the light entering the camera into the three primary additive colors—red, green, and blue—by using filters and three camera tubes (now chips). This created three signals: a red signal, a green signal, and a blue signal. These three signals were then combined into one signal, but each of the separate color components was placed out of phase so that they could be separated later at the receiver. Out-of-phase signals are related signals on a common path that are shifted slightly in time so that they may be kept separate in processing.

The color receiver has only one picture tube but three streams of electrons that strike the face of the picture tube, which is coated with groupings of dots of the three colors. When the three separate signals from the camera are fed to the three separate guns in the receiver, the original color is reproduced by the relative brightness of the three different colors of dots. Tubeless monitors now are replacing cathode ray tubes (CRTs). Liquid crystal display (LCD) and plasma display panels (PDP) are manufactured in large sizes for monitors and receivers and in miniature units for camera monitors.

Originally, color cameras and all color equipment were larger, bulkier, and much more expensive to manufacture and operate than existing black-and-white equipment. However, with the appearance of solid-state electronics, especially the MOS chips that replaced camera tubes, and now with digital signal processing and recording, color equipment is smaller, higher in quality, less expensive, and easier to operate than the black-and-white equipment of 35 years ago.

TV Optical Systems

Light passes through the lens to video transducers
(either chips or tubes).

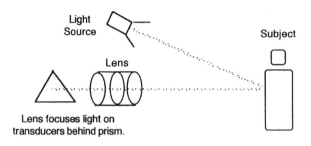

Light Source

Subject

Lens

Lens focuses light on
transducers behind prism.

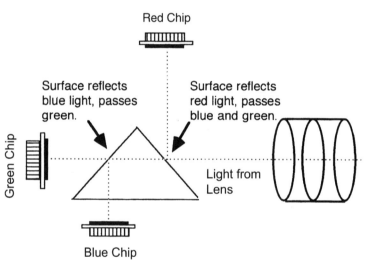

Red Chip

Surface reflects
blue light, passes
green.

Surface reflects
red light, passes
blue and green.

Green Chip

Light from
Lens

Blue Chip

Prism with special reflective coatings divides
colored light into three primary color
luminance values for conversion to electronics.

Measuring Video

To determine exactly how the camera is reacting to the light reflected from the subject, you need a precise means of looking at the electronic signal. The equivalent of an audio VU meter, a test instrument called an *oscilloscope* or *waveform monitor,* is used to monitor a black-and-white video signal. It converts the electronic signal into a visual equivalent that is calibrated for precise measurement. The scope can be set to look at one or two lines or at one or two fields at a time.

This electronic picture shows the sync pulses, their amplitude, their width, and their position in relation to other parts of the signal. It also shows the strength or level of the signal to indicate if the signal is too high (too much video amplifier gain or too much light coming into the lens) or too low (too little gain or not enough light). It also shows the relationship between the two major components of the signal: *gain* (white level) and *setup* (black level), sometimes called *pedestal.* These two signals must remain in the proper relative strength to each other to provide an acceptable picture.

In most newer cameras, the white and black levels are set automatically, but they may need to be adjusted periodically by a technician. The white level also is controlled by the iris setting in the lens. The ability to read and understand an oscilloscope is necessary only during a multiple-camera shoot and in the editing room.

The second type of video signal monitor is a *vector scope.* It shows the relationship of the three color signals—red, green, and blue. These three signals are deliberately set out of phase with each other; that is, each of the three signals starts at slightly different times (in fractions of microseconds). This out-of-phase condition is critical in converting the three black-and-white signals into one acceptable color signal. To make that adjustment, it is necessary to read a vector scope, which visually displays the phase relationships of the three signals. Once again, this is an internal adjustment in most field cameras. The ability to read and use a vector scope becomes necessary only with multiple-camera productions and in the editing room.

Digital video signals are much more complex and require complex testing equipment and oscilloscopes, which is beyond the scope of this chapter.

WAVEFORM MONITOR
AND VECTORSCOPE

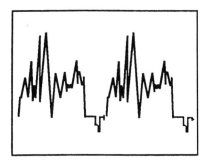

Waveform Monitor
(oscilloscope)

Electronic equivalent of
black/white (luminance value)

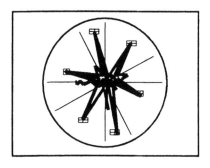

Vectorscope

Electronic equivalent of
color (chrominance and saturation values)

Digital Signal Standards

Between 1941 and 1967, three major video standards were set. The U.S. NTSC standard was accepted by much of South and Central America and also Asian countries aligned politically with the United States. Germany initially developed the PAL system, but it is used throughout the world in English-speaking countries and those countries aligned politically with the United Kingdom and their former colonies. France followed with Sequential Color with Memory (SECAM), which was adopted by former French colonies and some Eastern bloc countries. The major problem with these three systems is not their difference in quality but that they are incompatible; a program originating in an NTSC camera or recorded on an NTSC recorder cannot be viewed on either a PAL or SECAM receiver or played back on either a PAL or SECAM recorder. NTSC varies from PAL and SECAM in line and frame rates.

As digital television is becoming the standard around the world, plans to create a universal standard have failed. Currently, three international transmission digital systems exist: Terrestrial Integrated Services Digital Broadcasting (ISDB-T), developed in Japan; Terrestrial Digital Video Broadcasting (DVB-T), developed in Europe; and Advanced Television Systems Committee–digital television (ATSC-DTV), developed in the United States. In addition, the U.S. ATSC standard actually offers 18 different formats. The FCC refused to set specific technical standards, leaving the industry to decide among the available formats. Digital standards conversion equipment is available, but the equipment is expensive, and some loss in signal quality occurs during the conversion. With the continuing use of digital systems, the conversion between standards has become less of a problem.

The measurement of digital systems is based on the number of bits required to convert a signal from analog to digital. A bit is either an ON or an OFF signal, the basics of the binary digital system. The amount of memory (number of bits) required determines the quality of the conversion and the ability of a specific system to handle the number of bits. For example, 1 second of color video would require 28 megabytes of memory. To deal with that large amount of memory, most video signals are compressed. Compression is accomplished by using one of several Motion Pictures Expert Group (MPEG) systems that separate necessary information from redundant information to reduce the amount of memory required for any one segment or program.

The FCC will set a date that by 2009, all broadcasts in the United States will be in a digital format.

22

DIGITAL VIDEO STANDARDS

INTERNATIONAL DTV STANDARDS

SYSTEM/ COUNTRY	FRAME RATE	ASPECT RATIO	SCAN LINES	SCANNING
ISDB-T JAPAN	30, 60 fps	4:3, 16:9	480, 720, 1080	Progressive/ Interlace
DVB-T EUROPE	24, 30, 50 fps	4:3, 16:9, 9:4	480, 576, 720, 1080, 1152	Progressive/ Interlace
ATSC-DT NO.AMER	24, 30, 60 fps	4:3, 16:9	480, 720,1080	Progressive/ Interlace

US ADVANCED TELEVISION SYSTEMS COMMITTEE (ATSC) DTV FORMATS

FORMAT	SCAN LINES	ASPECT RATIO	FRAME RATE	US ADAPTER
HDTV	1080	16:9	24 P, 30 P, 60 I	CBS & NBC (60 I)
HDTV	720	16:9	24 P, 30 P, 60 P	ABC (30 P)
SDTV	480	16:9 or 4:3	24 P, 30 P, 60 P, 60 I	Fox (30 P)
SDTV	480	4:3	24 P, 30 P, 60 P, 60 I	None
LDTV	480	4:3	60 I	None

DIGITAL MEASUREMENTS

1 Bit = 1/8 Byte
1 Byte = 1/1000 Kilobyte (KB)
1 KB = 1/1000 Megabyte (MB)
1 MB = 1/1000 Gigabyte (GB)

8 Bits = 1 Byte
1000 Bytes = 1 KB
1000 KB = 1 MB
1000 MG = 1 GB

Pixel = smallest element of a picture
1 Video frame = 640 horizontal pixels × 480 vertical pixels = 307,200 pixels
1 Color video frame = 307,200 pixels × 24 bits of color = 7,372,800 bits or 921 KB
1 Video frame requires nearly 1 MB
1 Second of video = 30 frames = 28 MB of memory
1 Minute of video = 1680 MB or 1.68 GB of memory
60 minutes of video = 100 GB of memory
Most consumer computer hard drives are limited to 1 GB or less of memory.
Professional computers require increased amounts of memory for nonlinear editing.
Both consumer and professional systems use some form of compression to reduce the amount of memory required for processing and editing.

The Equipment

Background

The equipment currently used in single-camera video production has a relatively short history. In the early 1960s, a method of editing 2-inch quadraplex videotape was developed. Directors and journalists realized that some types of productions could be shot on one camera, recorded on videotape (even out of sequence), and then edited into a form suitable for airing.

By 1969, amateur videotaping became possible with the invention and sale of a Sony black-and-white vidicon handheld camera combined with an open reel ½-inch videotape recorder (VTR), later known as the EIAJ format. However, the early attempts at single-camera video production were primitive, primarily because of the lack of an adequate and efficient editing system.

In the mid-1970s, editing systems for both formats were developed, but the marketing of Beta and Video Home System (VHS) ½- and ¾-inch U-matic videocassette formats superseded the use of 2-inch and ½-inch EIAJ. The 2-inch format was difficult to edit, even with a computer controller, because it could not be still-framed for the precise location of edit points, and the quality of ½-inch EIAJ was below the technical level, warranting the further development of editing systems.

The original small-field cameras were developed for broadcast news operations to replace the 16-mm film equipment previously used by most stations and networks. News operations wanted small, lightweight equipment that could deliver broadcast-quality picture and sound instantaneously. Because such a system would be entirely electronic, the picture and sound also could be transmitted over microwave links for live coverage. In 1974, CBS was the first to successfully try such coverage, using a small camera and an early portable 1-inch helical VTR. The equipment was bulky and heavy compared with film equipment, but it provided the live picture required by news productions.

The development during the 1990s of smaller cameras using metal oxide semiconductor (MOS) chips feeding ½-inch, high-quality, digital videotape decks or recording directly onto computer memory, memory cards, or computer discs has moved the art and science of field recording to a greater level of quality at a lower cost. Editing these new signals can now be accomplished with laptop and desktop nonlinear editors, which provide shorter turnaround time between shooting and a completed news clip and make possible much more creative work on nonlinear editing equipment.

EARLY EFP EQUIPMENT

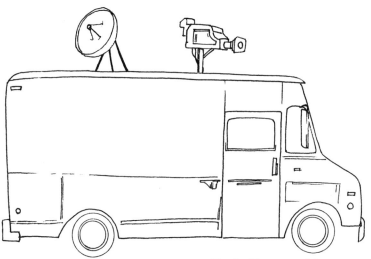

Early Remote Van
with Microwave Dish
and Studio Camera

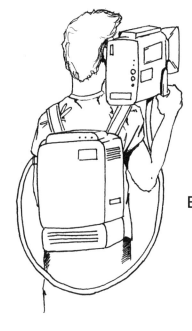

Early "Creepy-Peepy"
with Back Pack and
Handheld
Black & White
Camera

The Image Source: Tubes and Chips

Tubes

Until the late 1980s, all practical video cameras used an electronic tube to convert light to an electronic signal. Even though the quality and size of the smaller tube cameras made them applicable to both news operations and consumer use, the fact that they used tubes as light conversion transducers presented problems. The critical problem was their low level of light sensitivity compared with film. The average three-tube color camera has an equivalent ASA, or light sensitivity, of about $\frac{1}{100}$ of the faster film stocks. Also, tubes are susceptible to "burn," lag, and/or bloom. When a tube camera was pointed at a bright, high-contrast light source, such as the sun or a spotlight onstage, the surface of the tube was damaged; therefore, it would not accurately respond to normal light. The third problem with tube cameras was their sensitivity to loss of registration.

Chips

In 1984, the first video camera containing no tubes was produced. The light conversion tubes were replaced with all-electronic, charge-coupled devices (CCDs; also known as chips). CCDs are flat pieces of selenium and other light-sensitive metal crystal pixels. Instead of using a beam of electrons to scan the chip, the new technology uses a chip that is electronically read as light falling across its surface changes voltages. These changes become the electronic equivalent of the picture at the same frame and line rate as a picture tube. In addition, the signal from a chip can be exposed at a variety of frame rates and equivalent shutter speeds to produce slow- or fast-motion video, depending on the design of the camera.

The chips require a small amount of power, and because they are a flat piece of metal, they may be mounted directly to the surface of the light-splitting prisms inside the camera. This avoids any changes in registration between the chips, thus making the camera more rugged. The chips also are not prone to "burning" or aging as tubes were. Because the chips are solid-state components just like transistors, they last as long as any other component in the camera.

Currently, chips vary in size from $\frac{1}{3}$ to $\frac{3}{4}$ inch. The quality of the signal produced by the higher-quality chips intended for Digital Cinema approach that of 35-mm film for commercial and feature-length motion picture production.

Parts of Camera Chips and Tubes

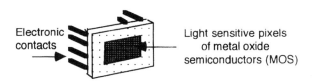

Electronic contacts

Light sensitive pixels of metal oxide semiconductors (MOS)

The heart of the chip camera, the CCD (charge-coupled device) sensor

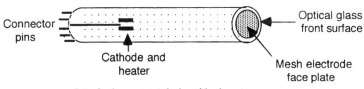

Connector pins

Cathode and heater

Optical glass front surface

Mesh electrode face plate

A typical camera tube's critical parts

29

Light Gathering

Optics and Focal Length

For a camera to operate, it must be able to concentrate light reflected from the surface of subjects to create an image. In current models of cameras, this function is provided by the *lens,* a series of optical glass or plastic elements cemented together and mounted in such a way as to focus light on the surface of the light conversion tubes or chips.

The lens is mounted permanently on the front of a consumer-quality camera. In equipment used at the professional level, interchangeable lenses may be used. The three basic characteristics of a lens are its focal length, its focus range, and its aperture settings.

Focal Length

The focal length of a lens is a measurement (usually given in millimeters) of the ratio between the diameter of the lens and the distance from its optical center to the focal plane (the location of the chip faces). The important factor to remember about focal length is that the longer the measurement, the greater the enlargement of the subject; the shorter the measurement, the smaller the subject will appear. Conversely, the longer focal length allows space for fewer subjects in the frame, and the shorter focal length allows more subjects to be included in the frame.

In addition, the longer the focal length, the more compressed the distance appears going away from the camera (called the *Z-axis*). Also, movement in front of the camera (the *X-axis*) appears to be accelerated. The apparent distances on the Z-axis using a short-focal-length lens appear to be increased, and movement on the X-axis appears to be slowed down. The focal length of a lens also determines its ability to focus over a range from close to farther away from the camera, called *depth of field.* Other characteristics of lenses determined by the focal length are explained later in this section.

FOCAL LENGTH

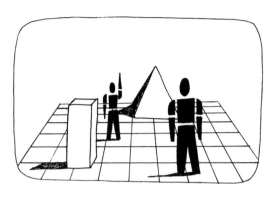

Long Focal Length:
subjects enlarged, fewer subjects in frame,
compressed appearance of distance

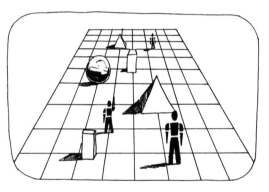

Short Focal Length:
subjects smaller, more subjects in frame,
increased appearance of distance

Light Gathering

31

Focus and Aperture

Focus

The ability of the lens to concentrate light reflected from a subject to create the sharpest image is called focus. Focus is a relative term, because a lens is in focus on an image when that image appears as sharply and clearly as possible on the surface of the chips. There are two separate ways to focus an image.

Front focus is achieved by adjusting (usually by turning the barrel of the lens) until the image is sharply focused at a point behind the lens, called the *focal point*. The second way to focus is the back focus. *Back focus* involves adjusting either the lens body or the pickup surface until an image located an infinite distance from the camera is in focus on the surface of the chips. The back focus is a technician's adjustment and should not have to be readjusted unless the camera or lens is jarred or bumped out of adjustment.

Focusing a zoom lens is more complex than focusing a prime or fixed-focal-length lens (which is used in feature film productions). The lens must be zoomed to its maximum focal length, framed and focused on the intended subject, and then zoomed back to the desired framing. All subjects located the same distance from the camera as the original subject will be in focus. Shooting any subject closer or farther away from the camera requires resetting the focus.

Aperture

The third basic characteristic of a lens is its aperture, or iris setting. To better control the amount of light that strikes the surface of the tubes or chips, an *iris,* or variable opening, is built into the lens. A numbering system was developed in the early days of photography and remains in use today—not only in photography but also in cinematography and videography.

The carefully calibrated sizes of the opening in the aperture are labeled with numbers called *f-stops*. Although the numbering system may seem strange, each full f-stop doubles (if opening) or halves (if closing) the amount of light allowed to pass through the lens. The f-stop number is the ratio of the focal length to the diameter of the aperture opening. The common full f-stops used in videography are f-1.4, f-2, f-2.8, f-4, f-5.6, f-8, f-11, f-16, and f-22. The term *stop down* means to close the aperture, or increase the f-stop number; to *open up* means to increase the size of the aperture opening, thus decreasing the f-stop number. An easy way to remember the change is to think of f-stops as fractions: $\frac{1}{22}$ is smaller than $\frac{1}{1.4}$.

FRONT FOCUS - BACK FOCUS

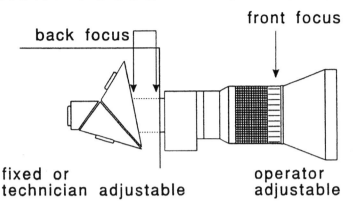

back focus

front focus

fixed or
technician adjustable

operator
adjustable

F-STOP OPENINGS

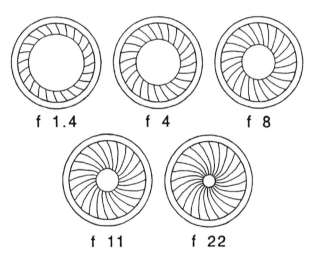

f 1.4 f 4 f 8

f 11 f 22

Depth of Field

Each of the previous characteristics of the lens—focal length, focus range, and aperture (f-stops)—is a tool to use in controlling the image desired by the videographer. Focal length affects how many subjects, how much of the subject, and the size of the subject in the frame. It also alters the appearance of subjects by distorting their size (see earlier discussion). Focus directs the attention of the viewer by placing important subjects in focus and less important subjects out of focus. Changing the focus, called *rolling* or *pulling focus,* can also guide the attention of the viewer from one subject to another. The f-stops must be set within the technical limitations of the camera and source of light so that there is enough light for the chips to create an image and not too much light that chips are overpowered. Changing the f-stop can alter the mood and apparent time of day. Slight underexposure can give the appearance of evening, early morning, or even nighttime or suggest a gloomy, dramatic mood. Slight overexposure can give the impression of bright daytime or lend a comic, lighthearted feeling.

A fourth characteristic of lenses, *depth of field* (DOF), is dependent on the three characteristics described previously. Depth of field is the distance from the camera that subjects appear in acceptable focus. This distance depends on the focal length of the lens, its focus setting, and the aperture opening. The longer the focal length, the closer the focus point; the wider the aperture setting, the shallower the depth of field. The converse is also true.

Depth of field is critical when trying to focus on close-ups or on rapidly moving subjects, such as in sports, and when light levels are limited. Depth of field also may be used creatively to exclude some subjects, by placing them out of focus but within the frame.

DEPTH OF FIELD

Increased
Depth of Field

Decreased
Depth of Field

Viewfinder and Accessories

To see what subjects you have included in your picture frame, you need an accurate viewfinder designed to accompany the camera. The viewfinder is usually mounted to the camera body so that the camera may be either handheld or tripod mounted.

A viewfinder is simply a small video monitor; it is similar to a home television receiver, except that it is wired directly into the camera and does not contain radiofrequency (RF) circuits to take signals from the air. Most cameras have small signal lights mounted inside the viewfinder hood so that you can monitor the operational characteristics of the camera without taking your eye from the viewfinder. Signal lights may indicate to the operator that the light level is too low, the tape is about to run out, or the battery is running low. In addition, an indicator shows when white balance has been achieved during the white-balance action.

Most viewfinders are mounted on the left side of the camera, making it difficult for a person who uses predominately the left eye to operate the camera. People who wear eyeglasses also may experience difficulty looking into the viewfinder. Some viewfinders on professional cameras can be rotated to the right side of the camera for operators who wish to use their left eye for viewing. Many viewfinders can be rotated into positions more comfortable for the operator if the camera is held under the arm or over the head.

The majority of viewfinders include contrast and brightness controls for adjusting the monitor in the viewfinder. These controls should not be adjusted except when the camera is either focused on a well-lit test pattern or is generating an internal test pattern called *color bars*. If adjustments are attempted while shooting anything other than a test pattern, the viewfinder may be incorrectly adjusted in attempting to compensate for a poorly lit subject. Most viewfinders provide only a black-and-white image for more accurate focusing, but newer flat-panel color monitors now are appearing on some models of professional and consumer cameras. Those same cameras provide a series of menus visible in the viewfinder enabling the operator to set camera and lens controls.

Digital Cinema Accessories

A video camera can be equipped with the same accessories a professional film camera uses when it is the camera for motion picture-type productions, such as commercials or feature-length films. Such accessories include a movable viewfinder, a matte box to hold filters or sun shades, remote controls for aperture and focus, as well as a video feed for the director to watch from a distance. This type of camera more than likely will be mounted on a dolly or crane to give the operator maximum flexibility in movement.

Camera Optical Viewfinder

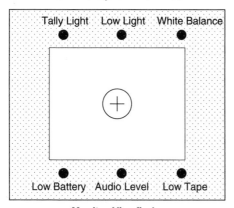

Monitor Viewfinder
Signal lights located inside viewfinder face

Camera Flat-Panel Viewfinder

9:16 Camera Monitor
Menus on the left, signal lights on the right

Camera Controls I

Each brand and model of camera and recorder may have different controls and, more than likely, different labels for the same controls. The description in this section uses the most common labels for the most common controls on both digital and analog cameras. The same controls described here, as well as others specific to a particular model of camera, may be accessible through the menus. Always consult your operation manual before attempting to operate any piece of equipment as complex as a video camera.

Bars/Gain Selector

The first control to set is the bars/gain selector. Generally, the two functions are combined on one control; however, on rare occasions, they may be separated. When the selector is set to "bars," color test bars appear in the viewfinder and are the output of the camera. You should record 30 to 60 seconds of bars at the head of each tape and at the start of each shooting session. This signal will be invaluable later for troubleshooting if there are problems with either the camera or recorder. The gain selector, which also may be labeled "sensitivity," provides a variety of increases in video gain in case light levels are too low for shooting at the normal gain position. The switch usually is marked with several steps: 6 dB, 9 dB, 18 dB, and so on. Each of these steps provides the equivalent of another f-stop of amplification. A negative consequence for the use of this control is the increase in video noise as higher gain is used. Video noise appears as a "crawling" on the surface of the picture.

Color Temperature Control/Filter Selector

A color temperature control designed to change the filters placed between the lens and the pickup chips may be labeled "filter selector." It usually is a wheel that holds a variety of filters. The color temperature control is accessible from the side or the front of the camera. Turn this wheel to select a particular filter or no filter. The no-filter position is intended for use indoors under incandescent lighting. For outdoor shooting, it may be either an 85 (yellow) filter, possibly labeled 5,600 K or an 85 + ND (neutral density) filter designed to add the yellow that is missing from the blue daylight. The ND filter added to the 85 compensates for bright sunlight, which might provide too much light for the video camera. In addition to those two positions, there may be several choices of different intensities of ND filters. There also may be an 80 (blue) filter, possibly labeled 3,200 K for interior tungsten correction, or an FL-M (focal-length-magenta) filter to help compensate for fluorescent lighting.

38

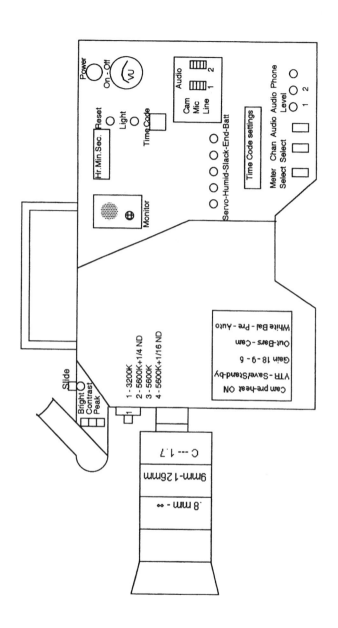

SONY BETACAM
Left Side

Power
On - Off
VU

Reset
Hr.Min.Sec.
Light
Time Code

Monitor

Servo-Humid-Slack-End-Batt

Audio
Cam
Mic
Line
1
2

Time Code settings

Meter Chan Audio Phone
Select Select Level
1
2

Slide
Bright
Contrast
Peak

1 - 3200K
2 - 5600K+1/4 ND
3 - 5600K
4 - 5600K+1/16 ND

Cam pre-heat ON
VTR - Save/Stand-by
Gain 18 - 9 - 6
Out - Bars - Cam
White Bal - Pre - Auto

C --- 1.7
9mm-126mm
.8 mm - ∞

Camera Controls I

39

Camera Controls II

White Balance

Once you have chosen the proper color temperature filter to match the lighting conditions for the shoot, the camera then must be white balanced. To do this, the camera is focused on a pure white source, generally a card or the back of a clean T-shirt, and then the white balance or auto-white button is held down for several seconds. Many digital cameras include a built-in automatic white balance that does not need to be set manually.

Some prosumer and consumer cameras may not provide any other operator controls. Higher-quality cameras also include the following controls:

- A *power selector switch* is used to indicate whether the camera has a battery mounted on it, is powered with its own separate alternating current (AC) power supply, or derives its power from the recorder's power supply or battery.
- A *VTR start switch* may be mounted on the camera body, but more than likely, it is mounted on the lens handgrip close to the thumb for easy use. This switch allows you to start and stop the recorder without leaving the camera or taking your eye from the viewfinder.

The following controls are usually located on the lens or lens mount:

- The *iris mode* control allows you to choose between setting the iris manually or letting the camera's automatic iris circuits set the iris.
- The *iris inst. control* is designed to allow you to zoom in on the surface that is reflecting the average amount of light for that scene, such as the face of the subject. Press the iris inst. control, which locks the iris at that setting, and then zoom back and/or pan to whatever framing is needed or to the beginning of that scene.
- The *zoom mode control* allows the operator to use the zoom function manually or use the motorized control of the lens to zoom.
- The *zoom lens control* is usually a rocker switch that allows you to press one end to zoom in and the other to zoom out. The harder you press, the faster the lens zooms. A gentle touch produces a slow, smooth zoom. Some cameras have an additional control to set the speed range of the zoom control from very slow to very fast.

One additional control may be mounted on either the lens or the camera body. The *return video* or *VTR return control* is a button that, when pressed, feeds the picture being played back from the tape deck into the viewfinder, allowing the videographer to observe the images previously recorded.

40

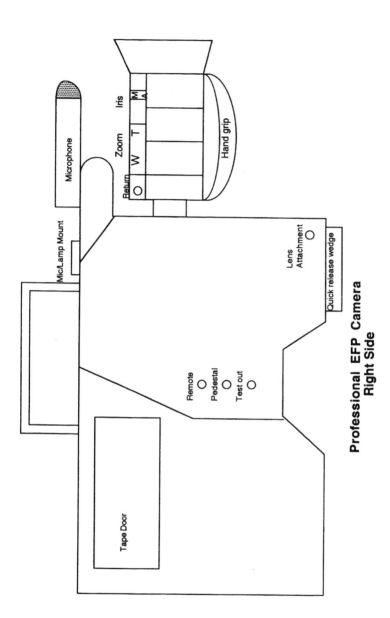

Microphone

Iris

M
A

Zoom

W T

Return

Hand grip

Mic/Lamp Mount

Lens
Attachment

Quick release wedge

Remote

Pedestal

Test out

Tape Door

**Professional EFP Camera
Right Side**

Camera Controls II

41

Camera Supports: Tripods

One of the first visual characteristics separating novice and professional videographers is the stability of the picture. Although many cameras may be handheld and most consumer cameras and some digital professional cameras are so small that a tripod seems redundant, a steady, controlled picture is essential for a quality video production.

The standard method of supporting a video camera is on a *tripod,* also called sticks. A tripod has three legs that are collapsible and individually adjustable in length to provide a solid, level support for the tripod head. The head is designed to fasten to the tripod and provides a system of moving the camera back and forth on a horizontal plane, called a *pan,* and up and down, called a *tilt.* In addition, high-quality tripod heads have a provision for precisely leveling the head by means of a leveling bubble built into the tripod. Most cameras are equipped with a plate that fastens to the bottom of the camera and is designed to snap easily onto the top of the head or snap off for easy removal.

The heads are manufactured in a variety of designs, depending on how expensive and how professional a piece of equipment the videographer requires. The critical factor in the design of heads is the method used to provide enough back pressure, or *drag,* so that a smooth, steady pan or tilt is possible. The method for creating drag separates the tripods designed for amateurs from those for professionals. The least expensive and most common heads for the consumer model tripods are friction heads that develop drag by the friction of two metal- or fabric-surfaced plates. It is difficult, if not impossible, to pan or tilt smoothly while recording with a friction head.

The next most expensive and higher-quality head develops its drag through a set of springs. In some designs with lighter-weight cameras, this system works well. The most suitable and expensive of this type is the fluid head. The movement of a thick fluid from one chamber to another creates drag in this type of head. This provides the basis for the smoothest and most easily controlled pans and tilts.

42

CAMERA SUPPORTS

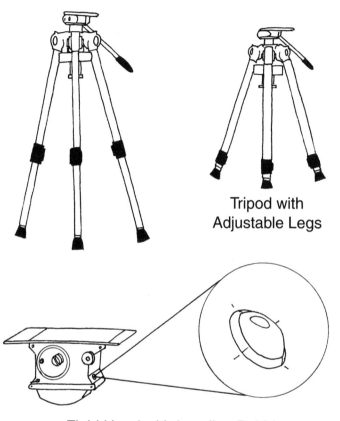

Tripod with
Adjustable Legs

Fluid Head with Leveling Bubble

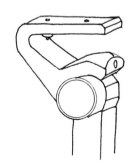

Spring-Loaded Head

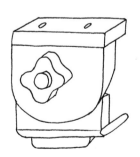

Friction Head

Other Camera Support Systems

In the professional world, many other support systems are used for single-camera production. These systems include *cranes, dollies, crab dollies, pedestals,* and *body mounts.* Most of these systems are expensive, bulky, and physically large. However, when needed, they do contribute a wide variety of potential movements to the director of a production. For a beginner, some of the same camera movements can be created by exploiting simpler pieces of equipment.

One way to move a camera while recording is to add wheels to the tripod, but this is not a stable or satisfactory method. A wheelchair or grocery cart provides a far more stable and easily controlled means of doing dollies and tracking shots. Sitting in a van and shooting out of a side or rear door is also a means of getting movement into a sequence. It helps to let a little air out of the tires. Hand-holding the camera in a moving vehicle—whether it is an automobile, airplane, helicopter, or boat—absorbs some of the shock and vibration, but the more the camera can be isolated from the movement of the vehicle, the better. Supporting the camera in a harness made of the heavy nylon or rubber bungee cords used by motorcyclists and truck drivers often yields flexible but vibration-proof support. Make sure the safety of the operator and the equipment are protected with appropriate precautions.

To duplicate a 360-degree crane shot, it is possible for the camera operator, camera, and tape deck to ride on a slow-moving merry-go-round. Riding in the bucket on a crane truck, such as those used by electricians and telephone installers, may allow you to capture a high-rising or lowering shot. A forklift with a platform large enough for a tripod and camera operator produces a limited pedestal up and/or down shot. Even riding up or down in a glass-sided elevator can supply a long vertical shot. Professionals use a low mount without tripod legs called a *high hat* to mount the head near the ground or on the hood of an automobile or boat. One method of duplicating this effect is to clamp the head to a heavy board (for example, a board 2 × 12 inches long). This board then is set either on the ground or clamped to the hood or deck. A safety rope is a necessity for this type of operation.

A body mount consists of a simple shoulder hook and pistol grip to hold the camera or a complex gyroscope-controlled, full-body case that encloses the camera operator's body. Such a mount allows the operator complete flexibility to walk, run, climb stairs, and turn in any direction without losing framing or disorienting the audience.

44

MOVABLE CAMERA MOUNTS

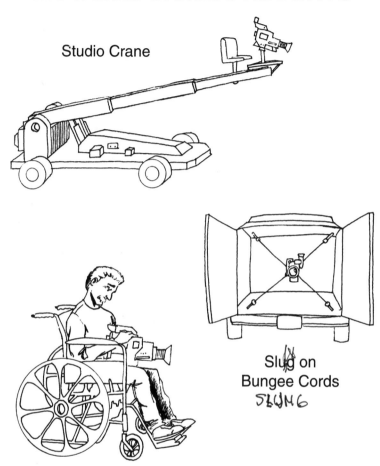

Studio Crane

Slug on
Bungee Cords

Handheld in Wheelchair

Hand-Holding the Camera

Many beginners and amateur videographers feel constrained by mounting the camera on a tripod or any other support. A much better production is possible with a stable support, but for those who cannot or will not use a tripod, following are some helpful hints on hand-holding a camera.

The first rule is to replace the tripod with your body, even though the body is only a bipod and a fairly unsteady one at that. By leaning against a third support to create a tripod, you can minimize the unsteadiness of hand-holding. Lean against a wall, post, automobile, building, or any other stable support to steady yourself.

Hold the camera firmly on your shoulder, with the elbows held tightly against the rib cage. The position that provides an even steadier platform than trying to hold the camera on the shoulder is one in which the camera is held under the right arm. This works only if the lower camera angle is not improper for that shot and is only possible if the camera's viewfinder is swiveled up so that you can look down into it. The new lightweight cameras are even more difficult to hold in a steady position. An extended shoulder mount provides some stability.

If a "walking shot" is attempted, remember that the professional body mounts are designed around gyroscopes that keep the camera pointed in one direction and level at all times. This gyro effect may be partially duplicated by using the body effectively. Hold the camera on the shoulder or under an arm; watch through the viewfinder; and move stiff-legged, swinging the body weight from one leg to the other. The swinging motion must be compensated for by swinging the camera an equal amount in the opposite direction so that it is always pointed at the subject. If the shot is supposed to be from the point of view (POV) of someone walking, then the slight weaving and bobbing is acceptable. If not, much practice will be necessary to make yourself a smooth "dolly" while hand-holding the camera.

When panning with the camera, place your feet in a comfortable position at the finish of the pan. Then twist your body into the starting position. This unwinding effect allows your body to relax as it approaches the end of the pan, rather than building tension and the shakes that go with such tension. This technique works similarly in a lengthy tilt. Position your body in a comfortable position at the end of the tilt, not at the beginning.

Remember, the human body was never meant to hand-hold a camera. Only through much practice, some additional equipment, and physical conditioning can a reasonably satisfactory shot be achieved by hand-holding.

HANDHELD CAMERA POSITIONS

On the
Shoulder

Leaning against
a Wall

Body
Unwinding to
Follow the
Movement

Sitting on the Ground

Underneath the
Arm

Hand-Holding the Camera

47

Analog Video Recording

The physical and electronic components designed to record and play back video and audio signals have been refined over the last 30 years to an amazing level of quality for an equally amazing level of cost, whether the signal is analog or digital.

As the video and audio signals pass from the camera to the recorder, the audio signal is fed to a recording head similar to the recording head on an audio tape recorder. The recording head is in a fixed position, and the audio signal is recorded in a longitudinal or continuous path on the edge of the tape stock. On the opposite edge of the tape, a signal generated inside the camera, called the control track, is also recorded using a fixed, longitudinal track. The audio signal may be embedded within the digital video as a PCM track.

Because the video signal is a much more complex signal and is recorded at much higher frequencies than either the audio or the control track signal, a different method of recording must be used. To record the high video frequencies, the relative speed of the record head passing the tape must be at a much higher speed than it is practical to record in a longitudinal or straight-line manner. Instead, the tape is wrapped around a drum containing one or more video recording heads that rotate inside the drum in the opposite direction from that taken by the tape as it is moving around the drum. The video heads barely project from the drum, touching the tape just enough to record the video signal in a series of slanted tracks across the tape. The tape is wrapped around the head in a helical shape, which is the source of one of the two common names for this type of recording: helical recording. The other term is slant track, an obvious reference to the pattern of video laid down on the tape.

Each video track contains all of the signals necessary for one field; therefore, if the tape deck is paused at any point, whichever field is wrapped around the drum is visible as the output of the recorder. In the pause position, audio cannot be heard and control track pulses cannot be counted because the tape must be moving across the playback heads for these two signals to be reproduced. Because it takes two fields to make a complete frame, when the picture is in pause, it is not an accurate reproduction of the recorded signal but it is sufficiently clear for editing purposes. If the re-coding is in the progressive mode, then each frame is visible in pause.

VIDEO RECORDING HEADS

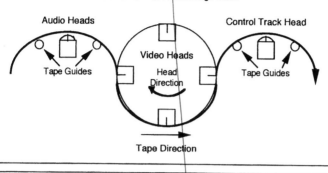

Location of VCR Recording Heads

Audio Heads

Video Heads

Control Track Head

Tape Guides

Head Direction

Tape Guides

Tape Direction

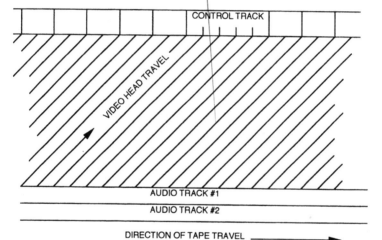

Video Tape Signal Tracks

CONTROL TRACK

VIDEO HEAD TRAVEL

AUDIO TRACK #1

AUDIO TRACK #2

DIRECTION OF TAPE TRAVEL

Digital Video Recording

The function of a digital videocassette recorder (VCR), whether as a separate unit from the camera or attached to the camera making a complete unit or camcorder, is to store the electronic impulses that represent the sound and picture created by the camera and microphone in the form of 1s and 0s, rather than as a continuously varying stream of electrons. The storage for a digital signal is not that much different than for an analog signal, but in many ways it is a much simpler signal to record. Despite its simplicity, the digital signal must be recorded in such a manner that the digital impulses may be easily retrieved in as close to their original form as possible. Digital recorders, whether they are recording an audio or a video signal, produce checking and compensating signals designed to correct any errors that may inadvertently have been recorded.

Before the video and audio signals pass from the camera to the recorder, they are converted into digital equivalents of the original signals. The audio signal is fed to a linear head, similar to the recording head on an audio tape recorder, or the signal is recorded with the video signal by extra audio heads mounted on the record drum. The audio signal then becomes a segment of the video signal. The control track, as in analog recordings, is recorded as a fixed, longitudinal track.

As in analog recorders, the tape is wrapped around a drum containing one or more video recording heads that rotate inside the drum in the opposite direction from that taken by the tape as it is moving around the drum. The video heads touch the tape just enough to record the video and audio signals in a series of segmented, slanted tracks across the tape. A digital tape in the pause mode appears the same as in an analog deck. A single field of each frame is viewed.

Because a digital signal is much more easily manipulated in both the editing and special effects operations, there may be a variety of built-in special effects in a digital camera that are not available on an analog camera. Some cameras allow editing dissolves and wipes within the camera, adding *pixilation* or other special effects while shooting. Most digital cameras are smaller, because the digital circuits are smaller and digital tape formats tend to be narrower, requiring smaller recorders. The development of disc recorders and digital camcorders allows instant entering of picture and audio directly from the camera to a computer equipped with a nonlinear editing program. High-definition television (HDTV) and standard definition (SD) vary in that an increase in the bandwidth is necessary to record HDTV, and there also is a difference in aspect ratio and line rate of the frame.

LINEAR & PCM AUDIO TRACKS

Linear Audio Track 1

Linear Audio Track 2 or Cue

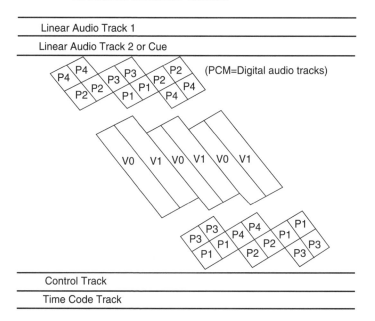

(PCM=Digital audio tracks)

Control Track

Time Code Track

**PCM & Linear Audio Tracks
on Digital Videotape**

Videotape Stock

The VCR, as opposed to the VTR, is designed to record video and audio material on magnetic tape encased in a cassette, rather than spooled onto an open reel. The cassette was developed not only for the convenience of the user but also as a means of protecting the sensitive surface of the tape stock from wrinkling, dirt, oil, and other contaminants, such as hair or smoke particles. The major disadvantage of confining the tape totally inside a cassette is that it makes splicing the tape for either editing or repair purposes difficult, if not impossible.

New blank tape purchased for recording is called *stock,* and it comes in a variety of forms and lengths depending on the tape format used. There is little difference among major brand names of new tape stocks, but there are some slight differences in quality depending on the type of tape—that is, whether it is high quality (HQ) or broadcast quality. The length of tape purchased should depend on how the tape is going to be used. Shorter tapes make for easier editing; longer tapes are necessary to record an entire program on one tape. Because the majority of the cost of the tape stock is the cassette itself, there is little difference in cost between a 5-minute and a 20-minute cassette.

It is important to handle cassettes carefully. Even though the tape is protected inside the cassette, care must be taken to avoid exposing the tape to smoke, dust, dirt, moisture, or excessive heat and humidity. Cassettes should always be carried in and stored in their cases in a temperature- and humidity-controlled environment. The handling of digital tape cassettes is the same as for analog tape. In some cases, however, digital stock is thinner and more prone to damage if mishandled, dropped, or stored improperly.

Video and audio signals now may be recorded on small digital discs that hold gigabytes of material. Signals also may be recorded directly on a built-in hard drive, removable memory stick, or removable solid-state chips to avoid the mechanical problems and power drain of a tape deck.

As soon as material is recorded, both the medium and the case should be clearly labeled, indicating the name of the contents, its length, and the date recorded. Taking care of such details early in the recording process can help prevent major problems later. It also provides a means of preventing both unwanted recorded footage from occupying storage space and critical footage from being accidentally erased or destroyed.

RECORDING MEDIA STOCK

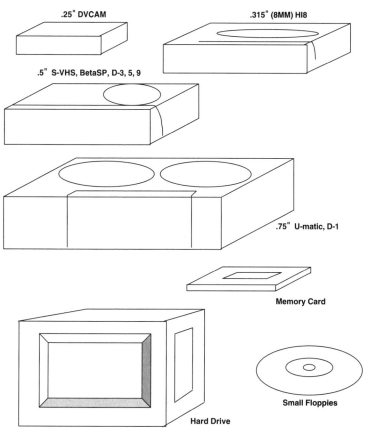

.25" DVCAM

.315" (8MM) HI8

.5" S-VHS, BetaSP, D-3, 5, 9

.75" U-matic, D-1

Memory Card

Hard Drive

Small Floppies

53

Videocassette Recorder Operation

Today's analog and digital VCRs are relatively easy to operate because their controls parallel those of the universal audiocassette recorder. Once the cassette is inserted correctly into the machine and power is applied, either from batteries or from an AC power adapter source, operation takes place through the familiar functions of record, play, fast-forward, rewind, and stop.

All tape decks contain some means of measuring the amount of tape that has been played or recorded. If the counter is set at zero when a new tape is loaded into the deck, it is possible to keep approximate track of where shots have been recorded on the cassette, thus enabling the operator or editor to find that same shot at a later time. Professional and higher-quality consumer tape decks measure tape usage with an actual timer that indicates the amount of time in minutes and seconds that has elapsed from the moment the timer was set to zero. If the tape deck is equipped with a Society of Motion Picture and Television Engineers (SMPTE) time code source, it indicates the location on the tape to the precise hour, minute, second, and frame.

Most recorders include a multipurpose meter and a switch that can be set to read the video level, audio level, or state of the battery charge. A switch that allows manual or automatic gain control of the audio is usually located near this meter. Several warning lamps may also be a part of the control panel of the tape deck. These indicate when the machine is recording or is paused, when the battery is running low, or when the tape stock is about to end. More advanced machines may include lamps that indicate high humidity, lack of servo lock, or other malfunctions of the machine.

Digital video disc (DVD) and compact disc (CD) decks may offer additional controls, such as skip, program, repeat, or pause. Some DVD controls appear on the screen and are accessed by scrolling through menus and choosing an operation.

Control Panels of Videotape Decks

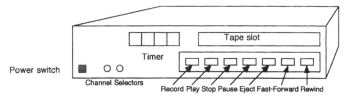

Power switch

Channel Selectors

Record Play Stop Pause Eject Fast-Forward Rewind

Connections on rear panel for RF in and out -
audio left and right in and out, and video in and out

Consumer Deck

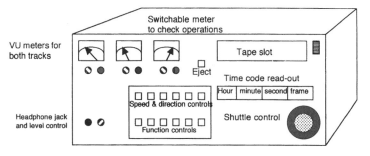

VU meters for both tracks

Headphone jack and level control

Connections on rear panel for each audio channel in and out,
usually at least two different video in and out, sync pulse,
computer connectors for editing controller, and time code
connectors. If a digital deck, both analog and digital in and out
connectors.

Professional Deck

Connectors, Plugs, and Jacks I: Power and Audio

Before any discussion of connecting equipment together, you need to understand the somewhat confusing world of cables and connectors. Unless a cable is permanently wired into a piece of equipment (e.g., microphone, camera, monitor, power source) the specific type of cable and specific cable connectors must be assembled and properly connected. The connector at either end of a cable is called a plug; the connector mounted on the wall or on the side of a piece of equipment is called a jack. There are both female and male plugs and jacks, and it takes one of each to make a connection. The contacts on a female plug are contained within the plug, whereas the contacts of the male plug project out. There are three major types of plugs/jacks: power, audio, and video.

Power Connectors and Plugs

Power connectors are designed to carry either 110/220-volt AC or 12-volt direct current (DC) power. Connectors for AC power are the same as the connectors on home appliances. Polarity and proper grounding must be maintained on all cables and plugs. Connectors for DC power may be either *DIN*, a special multipin *XLR* connector, or, for most VCRs, a special microplug used only for 12-volt DC.

Audio Connectors and Plugs

Professional microphone audio connectors are called XLRs, with a clip on the female plug or jack that either locks the plug to the jack or locks two plugs together. The clip must be released to separate the plug from the jack. XLRs are the best audio connectors to use because they cannot be unplugged accidentally and they contain three conductors, in addition to a shield for the best audio transmission.

Many manufacturers use a *mini-plug* (sometimes called a *⅛-inch phone plug*) or an *RCA plug* (sometimes called a *phono plug*). Both of these connectors are used for microphone and high-level audio connectors and can be easily mistaken for each other. However, they are not compatible, and damage can occur if an RCA plug is forced into a mini-jack or vice versa. Either of these plugs, mini or RCA, can be accidentally disconnected because they are held in place only by friction.

An older audio plug is the *¼-inch plug,* sometimes called a *phone plug* (probably because it was commonly used by the early telephone companies). It is easy to confuse the terms *phono* and *phone,* so it is preferable to differentiate audio plugs by the alternate terms listed previously.

56

AUDIO CONNECTORS

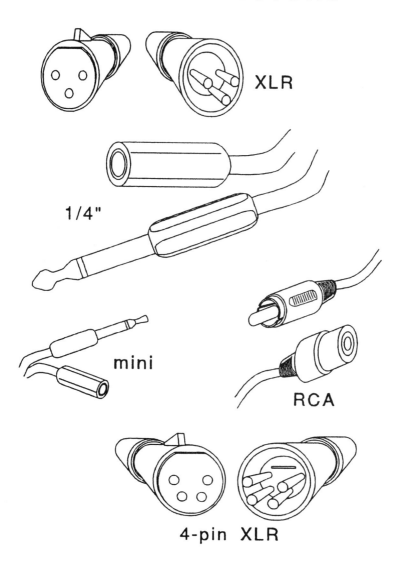

XLR

1/4"

mini

RCA

4-pin XLR

Connectors, Plugs, and Jacks II: Video

Six basic video plugs are in common usage today. The *RCA* connector, unfortunately, has become standard for consumer and some prosumer video equipment. Because it is a friction plug, it can be unplugged unintentionally and easily. It is also a common audio connector; thus audio cables may be misconnected by accident as well.

Professionals use a connector called a *BNC;* no two video specialists can agree on the derivation of this acronym. The most prevalent is "Bayonet Naval Connector," because it was first used by the navy. The BNC is designed so that it twists and locks into place, ensuring a secure connection, but it is still easy to connect and/or disconnect with one hand.

An older video connector is the *ultra-high-frequency (UHF)* connector. It has a threaded collar that is tightened once the plug has been inserted into the jack. Because the UHF connector is larger, more expensive, and more awkward to use, it appears on very few new types of equipment.

BNC, RCA, and UHF connectors are all designed to carry only the video signal and are all male connectors. If cables need to be connected together, a female adapter called a *barrel* must be used between the cables.

There are two methods of transmitting both audio and video information through the same cable. The first method uses separate conductors inside the cable for audio and video. The multipin camera and 8-pin monitor cables and plugs are examples of multiconductor cables. The second uses a special cable and connectors called *RF* or *F*. To use an RF cable, the audio and video signals must be combined into one signal using a circuit called a *modulator*. On the other end of the line, a *demodulator* must be present to separate the audio and video signals again. The RF connector is used by cable companies to connect their signal to a home receiver, and antennas are often connected with RF cables and plugs. The German *DIN* plug also is used on some European-manufactured equipment to carry both audio and video or only video or power voltage signals.

The *Separate VHS (S-VHS)* format carries video signals split into two separate signals, Y and C, for higher quality transmission of video. See the next section for digital cables and connectors.

VIDEO CONNECTORS

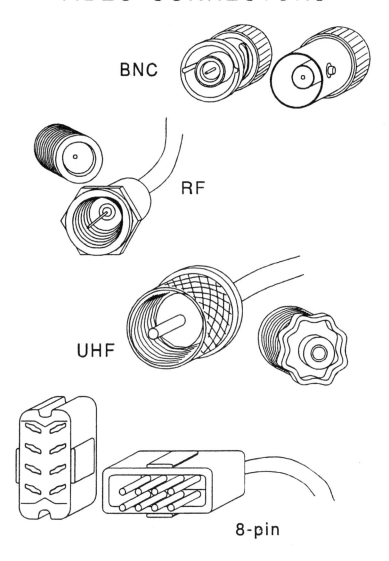

BNC

RF

UHF

8-pin

Connectors, Plugs, and Jacks III: Digital

Because digital signals are different from analog signals, an entirely new set of plugs, jacks, and cables needed to be designed and accepted by the industry. Also, because the digital world is still in a state of constant flux, new connectors and cables are designed and placed in use periodically, usually for new and specific uses. The S-VHS plug listed in the preceding section also may be used for Digital VHS (D-VHS) clrcults. DIN plugs also have been used for connecting computer peripherals to the main *central processing unit* (CPU) of a computer setup. Ethernet systems were designed in the 1970s, and they continue to be used for *local area networks* (LANs). The plug is similar to a standard telephone plug but is wider and has more bandwidth capacity. It is more useful than other cables for connecting equipment at greater distances without loss of signals. The standard telephone plug currently in use is also capable of carrying digital signals, when used in a *Digital Subscriber Line* (DSL), to feed broadband data down a telephone line. F and RF cables also carry digital signals, if the modulators and demodulators are designed for digital transmission.

A leading standard digital connector is the *Universal Serial Bus* (USB). Each end is shaped differently, but both are modified female connectors. The smaller end generally is connected to the peripheral, and the larger end is connected to the computer. Extension cables and breakout boxes designed to allow more than one cable to be connected to a single computer outlet makes this a flexible and much faster means of moving data from printers and keyboards than serial connectors and cables. A much faster system uses cables and connectors labeled IEEE 1394 (the official name; but it is also known as iLink and FireWire). It has 30 times more bandwidth than USB and can support up to 63 devices on one cable at distances up to 14 feet. There are two types of FireWire connectors: a 4-pin that often is used on camcorders and a 6-pin that usually is found connected to computers and hard drives.

As new equipment and types of services are designed and placed into use, there will be new connectors and cables systems. Pay close attention each time you connect or disconnect a cable to make certain you're matching the plugs and jacks properly. They are the weakest link in any system and are most prone to damage at critical stages of a production.

DIGITAL CONNECTORS

USB (Universal Serial Bus)

USB Peripheral Connectors

FireWire (IEEE 1394)
Left-Six Pin   Right-Four Pin

Left-Ethernet   Right-Telephone

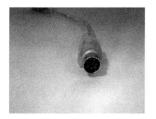

S-Video

Connector Panel: Consumer Model Recorders

The operational portion of a VCR that poses the most problems to the beginner is the connector panel. On a consumer-model recorder, it may contain a multipin jack for cable to the editor controller or to a computer, in addition to a variety of audio and video jacks, and either an AC power cord to plug into the wall or an internal battery pack.

Controller or Computer Cable Jack

The most obvious connector is the controller or computer cable jack, usually a multipin, serial, S-VHS, USB, or FireWire connector. These jacks may have guide slots or pins that match the cable connector to ensure that the pins and holes are properly aligned. To connect the cable jack, carefully align these guides, push in, and then turn the twist lock if that connector is a twist-type plug. Do not blindly insert the plug into the jack and twist until it mates. This method of alignment tends to twist and bend the small pins, destroying the plug or the jack on the equipment.

Some cables carry signals in both directions: from the camera to the deck; between decks; between a deck and a computer or editor controller; and, for monitoring, from the deck to a monitor. The cable also carries all of the control signals between the equipment.

Power Connector

A 12-volt DC connector, usually a microjack, may or may not be found on the connector panel if the deck is battery powered. Often, the 12-volt jack is located near the battery storage slot. Some decks, in addition to the micropower jack, may use either a 4-pin XLR or a 4-pin DIN jack for power sources.

Audio Jacks

Audio jacks are mounted on the panel for both input and output. The input jacks are either minis, RCA, or XLR jacks. If the format has two audio channels, there is an input jack for each channel or a stereo jack for both left and right channels. There should also be a switch to change the input level from microphone (mic level) to line level for each input jack. Audio outputs are usually RCA jacks, but in some cases, they may also be mini-jacks—again, one for each channel.

On most tape decks, an additional mini-output jack for headphones is usually provided. Often, this jack is a stereo mini-jack so that both audio channels may be monitored simultaneously.

62

PROSUMER DIGITAL VIDEOTAPE DECK

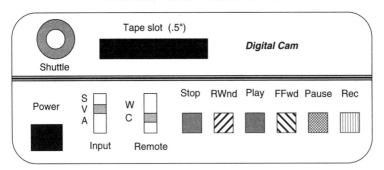

FRONT OF DECK

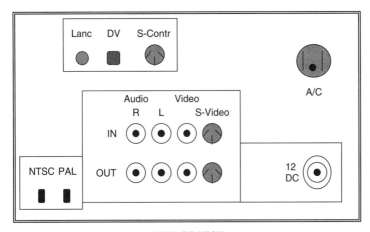

REAR OF DECK

63

Connector Panel: Professional Model Recorders

Video Inputs and Outputs

All of the jacks normally located on consumer equipment are also found on professional digital equipment. Additional connectors are described later. As newer types of equipment and signals are developed and added to production techniques, different inputs and outputs also need to be added. All decks have at least one video-input jack and one video-output jack. Other jacks may include a jack for a synchronization (sync) signal, if more than one camera is being used in a production, and a second video input and output pair; monitor; time base corrector (TBC) remote; 9- and/or 36-pin connectors; time code in and out; and a variety of audio jacks for inputs and outputs and for monitoring circuits. Digital signals require their own sets of connectors to ensure that digital and not analog signals are connected to digital inputs and outputs. Each jack has a specific purpose, and plugs should not be haphazardly connected without prior knowledge of the specific reason for the connection.

If the camera cable or connectors fail for any reason, a video cable can be run directly from the camera to the tape deck. This allows you to record video from the camera; however, audio and power lines have to be run separately, and the control signals between the camera and tape deck, such as the remote recorder start/stop, are not operable. In this situation, the camera must have its own batteries or other power source. Use of a single video cable to connect the camera to the recorder allows the two items to be much farther apart when weather or other production situations require such a separation.

Audio inputs can be either line or mic level. Make certain the proper connection and switch is thrown to match the proper choice. On some decks, there may be an RF connector. If the deck also contains an RF modulator within its circuits, then the combined audio and video signal is available at this jack. This signal may be viewed on a television receiver tuned to either channel 3 or 4 or may be fed directly into a consumer ½-inch deck. Digital decks will have digital signal inputs and outputs depending on the broadband requirements.

PROFESSIONAL CONNECTOR PANEL

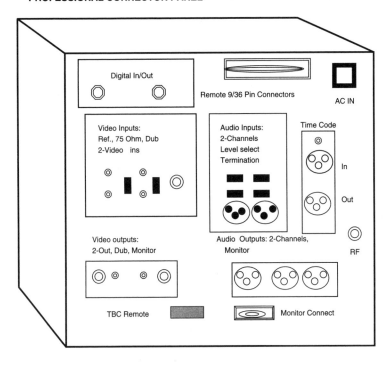

Digital In/Out

Remote 9/36 Pin Connectors

AC IN

Video Inputs:
Ref., 75 Ohm, Dub
2-Video   ins

Audio Inputs:
2-Channels
Level select
Termination

Time Code

In

Out

Video outputs:
2-Out, Dub, Monitor

Audio Outputs: 2-Channels,
Monitor

RF

TBC Remote

Monitor Connect

REAR PANEL PROFESSIONAL DECK

Connector Panel: Professional Model Recorders

Connector Panel: Separate and Attached Units

Separate Camera and Recorder Units

If the production unit uses a camera and a separate recorder, then they must be connected properly for each to function as desired. If the recorder and camera are designed to operate together, a single multi-conductor cable is sufficient. That one cable, generally with either a 10- or 14-pin connector, may carry power from the recorder to the camera and feed the video signal back to the monitor on the camera on playback from the recorder. The camera feeds a sync signal, the video signal, and the audio signal if the microphone is mounted or plugged into the camera. If the recorder and camera are not matched, an adapter cable may be needed to connect the two units. In most cases, the microphone or other audio inputs are connected directly to the jack panel on the recorder.

Attached Camera and Recorder Units (Camcorders)

There are two types of attached camera and recorder (camcorder) units: single piece and dockable. Single-piece units are manufactured so that the recorder and camera are one integrated unit, constructed on a single frame with all connectors between the camera and recorder hardwired internally. Dockable camcorders are designed so that the camera and recorder may be separated and even operated separately, if necessary. The dockable unit allows for more flexibility in the choice of either unit. For example, if a production does not require the highest quality of recording, the camera can be docked to a Hi-8 recorder. The same camera can also be used on a high-quality production simply by removing the Hi-8 deck and replacing it with a dockable BetaSP recorder.

Digital camcorders are manufactured as both single and dockable units. The digital units that record directly onto a computer disc are generally manufactured as single units to avoid mismatching digital circuitry between the camera and recorder.

The disadvantage to a single unit during an electronic field production (EFP) is that the loading and adjusting of the recorder may disturb the position of the camera. It is also more difficult for a continuity assistant to read time code from the camera than from a separate recorder. Also, if either unit fails, then the whole unit must be taken out of service, rather than simply removing the unit that failed.

CAMERA-RECORDER COMBINATIONS

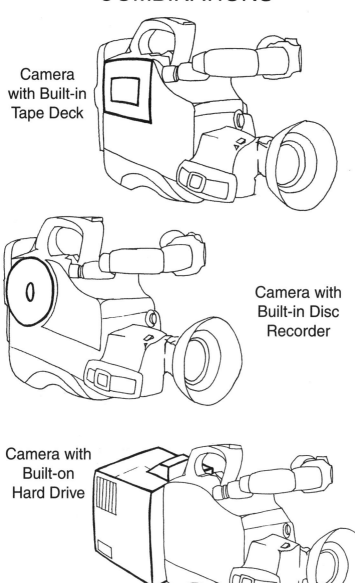

Camera
with Built-in
Tape Deck

Camera with
Built-in Disc
Recorder

Camera with
Built-on
Hard Drive

Audio: Cables and Connectors

In the past, audio had been the forgotten half of the audio/video production world. However, with the arrival of digital audio and increased audience awareness of the value of quality sound, audio production now has become much more important than in previous years.

Two developments in audio have contributed to the ability of production personnel to improve the quality of their audio: digital audio and the condenser microphone. Both have reduced the size of audio equipment and measurably increased its sensitivity and frequency response.

Digital Connections

Digital cables and connectors need to be chosen as carefully as those for analog signals. The square waves that make up digital signals are combinations of low and high frequencies, which require firm connectors to prevent leakage and cables designed to pass without distorting high and low frequencies. Lengths of digital cables also need to be considered in the design and installation of digital equipment.

Cables and Connectors

As with video cables and connectors, there is no universal standard for audio connectors. At the professional level, all mic-level audio connectors are XLR, three-contact-plus-shield, balanced-line cables and connectors. The signal is carried on the two internal wires, with the third wire connected to the shield. This system provides the maximum protection against outside audio interference and noise. Some professional equipment uses RCA (phono) plugs for line-level input and output audio connectors. This implies that the cable is a single conductor with shield and designed to operate with an unbalanced circuit. With line-level signals, the higher signal is less affected by outside signals. Some other audio circuits, such as headphones, may use a mini-plug as a connector.

Prosumer and consumer equipment may dispense with balanced lines and XLR connectors, using only RCA and mini-plugs for all audio circuits. The advantage of RCA and mini-plugs is their small size and low cost. However, their disadvantages—becoming easily unplugged and making poor electrical contact—far outweigh their advantages for professional use. An unbalanced line may pick up FM signals from nearby radio transmitters and noise generated by any equipment operating in either the audio frequency or RF ranges. An unbalanced mic line should be no longer than 5 to 10 feet to minimize picking up such noise and interfering signals.

Balanced vs. Unbalanced Lines & Connectors

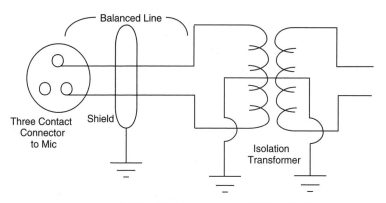

Balanced line and 3-contact connector (XLR)
Two internal shielded lines
grounded shield

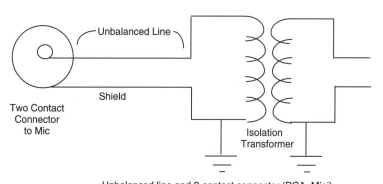

Unbalanced line and 2-contact connector (RCA, Mini)
One internal shielded line and
grounded shield
(May act as an antenna and pick up radio signals)

Microphone Types

Microphones are categorized in three ways: by their electronic impedance, by their element construction, and by their pickup pattern. In addition, microphone choices are also made on the basis of their specific
purpose or the type of audio pickup required.

Electronic Impedance

Microphones are classified as either *low* or *high impedance.* Impedance is
a complex measurement of resistance that also includes inductance and
capacitance. All professional mics are low impedance. A low-impedance
mic ideally should be connected to a two-conductor-plus-shield cable
and XLR connector. This allows connection to a balanced circuit, which
provides the best audio pickup. High-impedance mics are connected to
a single-conductor cable and either an RCA or mini-plug and should not
be used more than 5 to 10 feet from an amplifier.

Some consumer microphones are low impedance but are connected
to the recorder with a single-conductor, unbalanced line, which is a
compromise between professional low-impedance and consumer high-
impedance circuit connection.

Element Construction

The microphone element (transducer) types currently used are the
dynamic (moving coil), the *ribbon,* or the *condenser.* The dynamic mic is
the most common and most rugged, and for fast-moving coverage such
as news or documentaries, it provides the best frequency response for
the least cost. The pickup coil converts sound-wave energy to electric
energy without an outside power source or amplification.

The ribbon mic is intended for studio or booth use only because it is
heavy, large, and sensitive to movement, shock, or wind. It creates a fine
vocal quality, especially for the male voice. Its *transducing* element is a
thin, corrugated ribbon suspended between the two poles of a heavy
magnet. A ribbon mic can be used on EFP shoots if the environment is
controlled and the mic is kept out of inclement weather. The condenser
microphone is gradually replacing most other types of mics. Originally, it
was expensive, heavy, and large, and it required amplifiers and power
supplies located adjacent to the mic. With solid-state circuits and mini-
preamplifiers powered by small batteries or by current supplied from the
amplifier *(phantom power),* the condenser mic has become much more
practical. With its built-in preamplifier, it is sensitive, has a fine frequency
response, and is small and lightweight.

MICROPHONE ELEMENTS

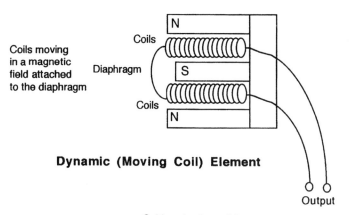

Coils moving in a magnetic field attached to the diaphragm

Coils

Diaphragm

Coils

N

S

N

Output

Dynamic (Moving Coil) Element

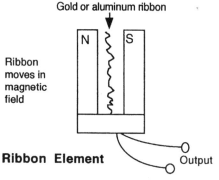

Gold or aluminum ribbon

N   S

Ribbon moves in magnetic field

Output

Ribbon Element

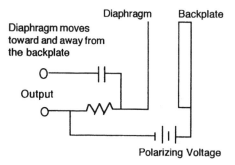

Diaphragm moves toward and away from the backplate

Diaphragm

Backplate

Output

Polarizing Voltage

Condenser Element

Microphone Pickup Patterns

There are three basic pickup patterns: bidirectional, omnidirectional, and unidirectional. *Bidirectional* mics have little use in field productions and are best reserved for studio productions. If the shoot is staged in a controlled environment or interior location, a bidirectional mic may be used for interviews. Its name is derived from its ability to pick up sound from two sides equally while suppressing sound from the other two sides.

Omnidirectional mics pick up sound from all directions, 360 degrees around the mic, with nearly equal sensitivity in all directions. All EFP audio kits should contain at least one good omnidirectional mic for crowd pickup and ambient noise recording.

The general background ambient noise of a location is called either wild or nat (short for "natural") sound. *Wild* or *nat sound* is useful material to record for later application in editing to provide an audio transition between scenes and to create the atmosphere of the original location for later voice-over narration.

The most useful mics are those that are derived from the unidirectional mic. A true *unidirectional* mic picks up sound only from the end of the mic. An extreme example of a unidirectional mic is a *shotgun* mic. It is designed to have a very narrow (as narrow as 5 degrees) pickup pattern. Its sensitive area is predominately straight out from the mic, but there are nodes or areas to the side and behind within which sound also may be picked up; this cannot be avoided, even with the best and most expensive shotgun mics. The audio kit of any EFP operator should contain several shotgun mics of various lengths and pickup patterns.

The *cardioid* mic is a special type of unidirectional mic designed to combine the pickup pattern of the unidirectional and omnidirectional mics to create a heart-shaped pattern in front of the mic. This provides the ideal pattern for an interviewer to hand-hold a mic between two people, to use the mic while describing an event without picking up too much background noise, and to use as a close-miked shotgun. If only a single mic may be carried, then a cardioid mic is the best choice.

Some professional microphones are designed with variable directional settings; they may be adjusted with a switch on the case to be omnidirectional, unidirectional, or cardioid. As with all equipment, multipurpose electronic equipment seldom performs as satisfactorily as equipment designed to perform a specific function.

The output of all microphones is an analog signal. The analog audio signal may be converted to a digital signal either in the preamplifier or in a digital-to-analog converter located later in the signal stream.

Microphone Pickup Patterns

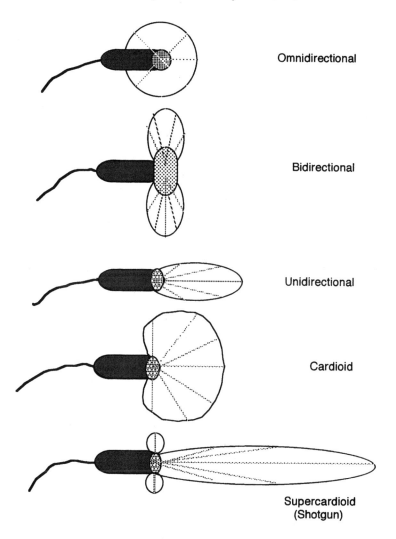

Omnidirectional

Bidirectional

Unidirectional

Cardioid

Supercardioid
(Shotgun)

73

Microphone Mounting

Microphones may be mounted at the end of a small handheld boom called a *fish pole;* on a small, movable, tripod-mounted boom called a *giraffe;* or, if space allows, on a large wheeled boom that the operator rides on called a *perambulator.* The type of mic usually mounted on booms is a cardioid or short shotgun. The mic can be hung from a gaffer hook from the ceiling; from a hanging light fixture, door, or window frame; or from any other stable piece of tall furniture in the room. Another method of mic placement is to hide it behind objects between the talent and the camera, for example, floral arrangements on a table, books, telephones, or any other set piece large enough to hide the mic and its stand. A third method is to place a unidirectional mic on the body of the subject. The mic may be attached in plain view, hanging from the neck as a lavaliere, or a smaller peanut mic may be attached under the talent's necktie, shirt, or blouse or to a jacket lapel.

The mic may be wired directly to the recorder, or it may be a wireless mic feeding a small transmitter hidden on the body of the talent and picked up by a small receiver wired to the recorder. Wireless mics are becoming more popular as their price and their sensitivity to other RF signals in the area are reduced. Current transmitters are designed to be smaller and more powerful, correcting many of the previous problems.

Each individual production requirement determines the best type of mic for that situation. Follow general recommendations listed in this section and in other books and articles on microphone usage and placement.

For some field productions—sporting events, game shows, and live coverage of nonvideo events—the microphone need not be hidden. Those situations allow you to place the mic or mics in the best position for maximum quality and sensitivity of audio pickup. The mic should be placed in direct line with the performer's mouth, below the face, and depending on the type of microphone, approximately 12 to 15 inches from the mouth. The microphone should be close enough for clear pickup and the exclusion of unwanted sounds but far enough away to avoid picking up the popping of Ps and other plosive sounds.

In addition, the mic should be placed so that its pickup matches the approximate perspective of the picture. If it is an extremely wide shot, then the audio should sound off mic; if it is a tight close-up, then the pickup should be intimate and close-miked. Often, the type of environment—a closed-in small room; outside in an open space; or a large, echo-filled auditorium—partially determines the best choice of microphone.

MICROPHONE MOUNTING DEVICES

Lavalier   Lapel

Table Stand

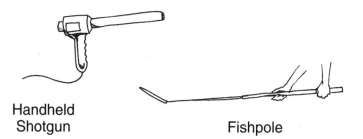

Handheld
Shotgun   Fishpole

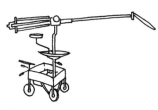

Perambulator

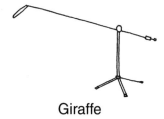

Giraffe

Audio Recording Considerations

Non-miked Audio Sources

In addition to recording audio from microphones, you may find it necessary to record non-miked audio sources. Such sources may be the output of amplifiers, public address systems, or tape or disc decks. Each of these sources produces high-level output and needs to be fed into a high-level, high-impedance input on the recorder. Matching impedance and level is critical for a satisfactory recording. Check the output specifications of the high-level source and match it to the specifications of the recorder being used. If they do not match, a matching transformer or amplifier should be inserted into the circuit to guarantee a proper match. If not closely matched, either the audio will be badly distorted or the level will be too low for any practical use.

Which Audio Track to Use

Another consideration is the choice of audio channel to record on the videotape. All professional videotape machines offer more than one track for audio recording.

Prosumer videotape formats such as older Hi-8 and the newer DVCam formats also have audio tracks recorded in different positions on the tape stock. These formats now record the audio digitally within the video signal, as well as on longitudinal tracks. The digital tracks are usually stereo and are very high quality, but they are difficult to edit on linear editing systems because they are part of, and cannot be separated from, the video signal. However, they can be edited and dubbed to a longitudinal track on another tape for editing. (This process results in a loss of quality in the process unless each generation is in a digital format.)

Audio pickup, whether it is analog or digital, is often ignored or thought of last; in reality, however, audio often carries more than half the critical information in a story. Therefore, it is important to plan for and spend time properly setting up microphones, mixers, and cables and choosing audio channels for the best possible audio recording together with the video recording.

TRACK LOCATIONS ON VIDEOTAPE FORMATS

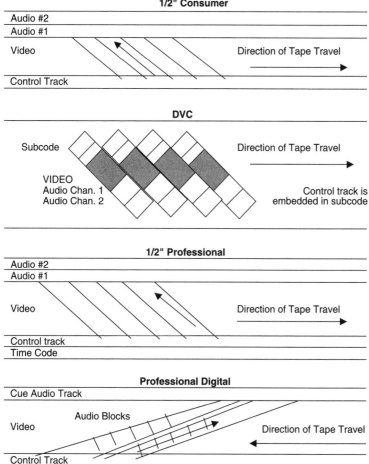

1/2" Consumer

Audio #2

Audio #1

Video   Direction of Tape Travel

Control Track

DVC

Subcode   Direction of Tape Travel

VIDEO
Audio Chan. 1   Control track is
Audio Chan. 2   embedded in subcode

1/2" Professional

Audio #2

Audio #1

Video   Direction of Tape Travel

Control track

Time Code

Professional Digital

Cue Audio Track

        Audio Blocks

Video   Direction of Tape Travel

Control Track

Time Code

77

Lighting Instruments

The function of lighting at its simplest level is to provide enough illumination so that the camera can reproduce an image. The complexity of lighting and lighting techniques is drawn from the need for the instruments to serve the aesthetic needs of the medium—that is, to set mood, time, and location and to draw attention to the critical portions of the frame.

Lighting instruments have evolved from both the stage and motion picture industries, just as most audio equipment has evolved from the radio and motion picture industries.

Floodlights

Three basic types of field lighting instruments exist: *floodlights, focusing spotlights,* and *fixed-focus instruments.* Floodlights provide a broad, relatively uncontrolled, soft, diffused light used to cover large areas and fill in shadowed areas. The most common field floods are softlights, broads, and umbrella lights. *Softlights* are the largest type, but, constructed of folding aluminum frames and cloth reflector covers, they are portable. *Broads* are smaller, boxlike instruments usually equipped with a barn door to control the coverage of light; they often contain only one lamp. *Umbrella lighting* is more of a technique than a specific type of instrument, because any spotlight can be fitted with an umbrella. The concept of umbrella lighting is to focus light from a spotlight onto an umbrella-shaped reflector mounted on the instrument so that light strikes the inner concave surface of the umbrella and is reflected back in the opposite direction.

Fluorescent lighting uses specially designed tubes that radiate light within a reasonable range to match the Kelvin temperature of either daylight or tungsten.

Focusing Spotlights

Focusing spotlights are either open faced without a lens or have a *Fresnel* (pronounced Frez-nel) or *plano-convex* lens. Focusing spots are essential for critical creative lighting.

Fixed-Focus Instruments

Fixed-focus instruments are designed around a lamp similar to an auto headlight. Their main purpose is to light a wide area with an even but controlled field of light. The lamps are called *FAY* if the output is 5,400 K and *PAR* if the output is 3,200 K (see "Color Temperature" later in this chapter). All of the instruments discussed in this section are designed to operate from portable floor stands and may be powered by 110- or 220-volt AC power. They also can be mounted from a variety of gaffer mounts on walls, doors, or other sturdy objects.

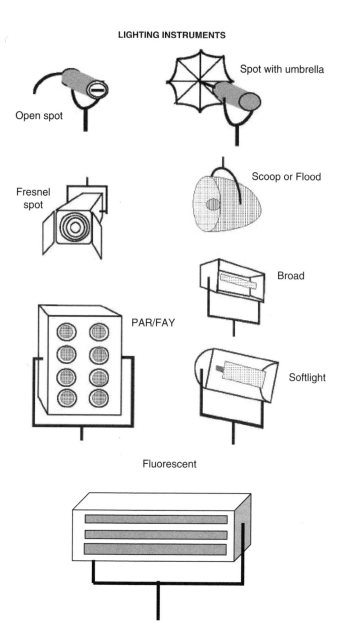

Spot with umbrella

Open spot

Fresnel spot

Scoop or Flood

Broad

PAR/FAY

Softlight

Fluorescent

Controlling and Powering Light

Controlling Light

Because field production seldom allows for the use of a portable light dimmer board, control over the light output becomes critical for creative shooting situations. Two simple, portable techniques are used: reflectors and tents. *Reflectors* are large foam boards covered on one side with a variety of surfaces—plain white, colored, or textured. These reflectors are used to throw a soft fill light into areas not easily reached with instruments or to provide light when an instrument is not available or would cast an additional shadow. *Tents* diffuse light, allowing the use of a number of instruments without creating unwanted shadows.

An EFP lighting kit should contain a set of gaffer's accessories: gobos, clamps, stands, weights, brackets, reflectors, and gaffer tools. A *gaffer* is a lighting technician. Among the equipment used by a gaffer are pieces of fabric used to block light, called *gobos,* and electrician's tools such as wrenches and pliers.

Power Sources

For field production, there are three sources of power: the AC present in most buildings, batteries, and portable generators.

Portable generators are expensive, noisy, and for video cameras, an uncertain source of stable power. The instability presents no problem for lighting directors, but the noise and expense might present problems for the producer, director, or both. Batteries for electronic news gathering (ENG) crews are becoming more dependable and longer lasting for most EFP production situations, but they require care in handling of charging and discharging. ENG is a specialized form of single-camera video production. ENG crews work in a variety of locations where electrical power is not readily available; therefore, they must rely on batteries.

The most dependable source of power for lighting is the AC circuits in most buildings. Because lighting instruments draw much more current than any other piece of equipment, some knowledge of wattage, current, and voltage is necessary. Standard power in the United States is delivered either at 110 or 120 volts. The lamps in lighting instruments are rated in watts, and the rating on power circuits in buildings is in amperage (amps). You can perform the simple translation of watts to amps or vice versa by using Ohm's Law: wattage = voltage × amperage. If voltage is treated as a constant of 100 (this provides a built-in 10% safety margin), then to find wattage, simply multiply amps by 100. To find amps from known wattage, simply divide wattage by 100. Both calculations can be done easily without a calculator.

80

APPLICATION OF OHM'S LAW TO TYPICAL LIGHTING SET-UP

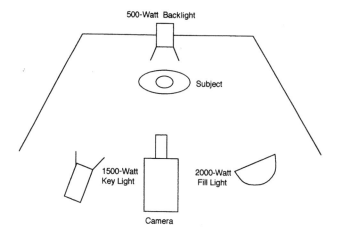

OHM'S LAW: WATTAGE = VOLTAGE x AMPERAGE
W = V x A

Assume V = 100 V as a constant

To find Amperage: $A = \dfrac{W}{100}$

To find Wattage: W = A x 100

In the example above: Backlight =   500 W
Key Light = 1500 W
Fill Light = 2000 W

TOTAL = 4000 W

Amperage = $\dfrac{Wattage}{100}$

Amperage = $\dfrac{4000}{100}$

Amperage = 40 A

Color Temperature

The final consideration in lighting equipment actually is a part of the camera operation, but the problem starts with the source of light. All light sources are not equal in their actual color. The human eye and mind compensate for this variation by creating the illusion that light within a certain range appears white. Actual measurement of the color of light is in degrees Kelvin, based on the color of a carbon heated and measured at certain temperatures. The lower the Kelvin temperature, the more reddish yellow the light appears; the greater the Kelvin temperature, the bluer the light appears.

There is no actual "white light" on the Kelvin scale. Typical candlelight measures less than 1,800 K. An ordinary incandescent light bulb measures 2,800 K. Professional tungsten-halogen lamps measure 3,200 K. Daylight varies from approximately 4,000 K to more than 12,000 K, but the standard is considered 5,400 K. The lower the Kelvin temperature, the "warmer" the color is; the greater the Kelvin temperature, the "cooler" the color is.

The critical factor concerning the color temperature is that a camera sees and reproduces the actual color of the light source as it is reflected from the subjects. An electronic camera can be adjusted to compensate for any variation in the color temperature by the process of white balancing. To light a scene properly, though, it should be lit with consistently color-balanced light sources.

Professional lamps are accurately rated for their color output, but when shooting in the field, you may be in an environment where the light sources are not controlled. Home incandescent lighting is warmer than studio lighting; office fluorescent lighting is bluer and greener than other lighting. (Normal consumer fluorescent lamps do not have a specific Kelvin temperature because they are a pulse light.) If you are shooting next to a window, the daylight entering the window does not match the color temperature of the production lamps. This situation is called mixed lighting.

When arranging lighting, it is necessary to take into consideration the color temperature of the available light sources by measuring them with a Kelvin temperature meter or by arranging to have all light sources be of the same color temperature.

Fluorescent light does not emit a specific color temperature but can be filtered either at the camera or on the tubes themselves to correct the temperature to match the camera settings. Newer fluorescent tubes that have been designed to match 5,400 K are currently available.

COLOR TEMPERATURE OF LIGHT SOURCES

Color Temperature	Light Sources
1,850 K	Open flame
2,000 K	Worn household lamp Sunrise, sunset
2,800 K	Unshaded new household lamp
3,200 K	Quartz-Halogen studio lamp
3,400 K	Photoflood lamp
4,250 K	Early morning, late afternoon sunlight
4,800 K*	Fluorescent lamp
5,000 K	Carbon arc lamp
5,400 K	Noon sunlight
5,600 K	HMI lamp
6,000 K	Overcast sunlight
8,000–20,000 K	Direct blue sunlight

*Fluorescent lamps are pulse lamps and do not emit a specific color temperature, but do emit light with a high blue–green content that may be compensated for with proper filtering.

Color Temperature

Measuring Light Intensity

In addition to measuring the Kelvin temperature of the light sources to attain the best lighting, you must measure the intensity of the light sources and the light reflected from the subjects.

The measurement of the light from the light sources *(incident light)* is accomplished by pointing an incident light meter at the light source. The measurement of the light from the subject *(reflected light)* is accomplished with a reflected light meter pointed at specific areas of the subject.

The two methods of taking light-level readings are required to determine the two types of lighting ratios necessary for quality lighting.

Lighting Ratio

Some minimum amount of light is required to produce an acceptable picture, called base light. An incident light reading of the amount of light falling on the subject gives the lighting director two pieces of information: the base light level necessary to produce an acceptable picture, and the ratio of fill light to key light. By pointing the meter at the lights from the subject's position with just the fill light turned on and then taking another reading with fill and key lights on from the same position, a numerical ratio, called the lighting ratio, is determined. The standard starting lighting ratio is 2 : 1; that is, there is twice as much light from the key and fill as from the fill alone. A backlight ratio may also be taken and should be close to 1 : 1; that is, the backlight should approximately equal the key light.

Contrast Ratio

The measurement for *contrast ratio* is a little more complex. A reflected spotlight meter is needed to measure accurately the amount of light reflected from the brightest object in the picture and the light reflected from the darkest object.

If the amount of light reflected from the brightest portion of the frame in which detail is necessary reflects more than 30 times more light than the darkest areas needed for detail, more fill light will be needed on the darkest areas or some light will have to be taken off the brightest areas.

Carefully lighting for the contrast range of the video camera should prevent areas from "blooming" or "flaring" into a white mass and keep important areas from appearing so dark that they look "muddy."

Digital cameras can accept a slightly broader range of contrast than analog cameras, but because a digital image will show much more fine detail, lighting must be accomplished to a finer level.

84

BASIC THREE-POINT LIGHTING PLOT
WITH MEASURING POSITIONS

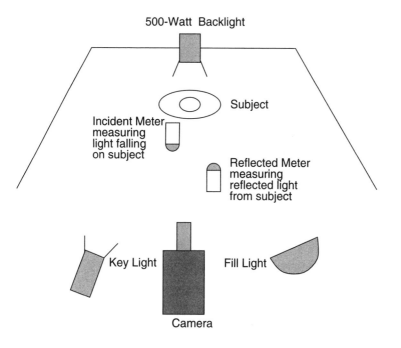

500-Watt Backlight

Subject

Incident Meter measuring light falling on subject

Reflected Meter measuring reflected light from subject

Key Light

Fill Light

Camera

The Production Process: Preproduction

The production process is most easily understood and organized by its three steps: preproduction, production, and postproduction. Each step involves specific functions and operations that are critical to the final production.

Preproduction Planning I

Before any serious work can begin on a video project, a source of funding must be found. An interested party must commit money for staff, crew, cast, research, facilities, equipment, and expendable materials. Such sources of funds may be clients who have contracted for the specific project, such as television stations or networks, cable networks, or funding agencies; government agencies; money-lending agencies, such as banks and savings and loan companies; or insurance companies.

Proposal

Regardless of the funding source, there is common information that must be supplied to gain access to such funding. The first document of the preproduction process is called a proposal. A proposal generally is the responsibility of the producer, but it is better to prepare it with the assistance of the writer(s) and director. Considerable knowledge of the subject is imperative to avoid mistakes, misinformation, or serious inaccuracies. A complete site survey, interviews, and library and other research must be carried out before the proposal can be written.

After the research has been completed, all of the information is organized into a concise, meaningful package that briefly explains the objectives of the production, the target audience, and the distribution methods. Key production factors, basic style and genre, unusual production techniques, and special casting and location considerations, together with the length, recording format, and release format, all need to be explained in easily understandable lay terms. The proposal writer must be accurately aware of how the completed production is to be distributed, such as on videotape; broadcast or cablecast; or converted to a digital format on tape, CD-ROM, or computer disc. The proposal writer must understand that the person reading the proposal and making a funding judgment may not have a media background. The proposal must be written so that all aspects of the production are presented clearly, avoiding production jargon.

An approximate timeline and budget complete the proposal package. Both of these should be prepared carefully and realistically. Too much or too little of either can discourage a client or funding source. Worse yet, a miscalculation in either section can place the producer in a position in which it is impossible to complete the project because of insufficient funds or time.

88

SAMPLE PROPOSAL FORMAT

TITLE:	Safety Training	PAGE:	1
WRITER:	T. Bartlett	LENGTH: 10 mins	
CLIENT:	Mountain Industries	DATE:	10-10-04

Rivers and Streams Productions, Inc. will produce a ten minute, color videotape to be used as a training medium for new and present employees of Mountain Industries. The tape will target specific safety procedures necessary to be followed in the unique operation of logging in the mountains of Montana. The tape will emphasize personal safety actions and procedures required by the Occupational Safety and Health Administration.

The shooting schedule will last for ten days, weather and other acts of nature notwithstanding. Postproduction will last for four weeks following the completion of principal videography. Taping will start within two weeks of final script approval. Research and preparing of the treatment will last three weeks following the acceptance of the proposal. The final script will be prepared within three weeks of acceptance of the proposed treatment.

The budget will be approximately $35,000.00, depending on specific technical requirements of the script. Because the script calls for a series of dangerous actions requiring stunt actors and technicians, some allowances for costs and shooting overruns may be required.

The format will be semi-documentary/instructional with the tape narrated and techniques explained by an actor representing a skilled and knowledgeable logger. Both incorrect and correct operational procedures will be illustrated. Employees, equipment, and facilities of Mountain Industries logging operation will be required for the production of this tape.

Preproduction Planning I

Preproduction Planning II

Treatment

After the proposal has been written, a treatment must be prepared. A treatment is a narrative description of the production. Like the proposal, the treatment is intended to be read by the potential financial backers to assist them in making the decision as to whether they are willing to entrust their money to the producer.

The first paragraph of the treatment repeats key information from the proposal: title, length, format, and objective of the production. The treatment should be written as if the writer is describing what he or she sees when watching a playback of the completed production. Dialogue is not used, but indications of the type of conversations or narration should be included. Also, technical terminology such as "dissolve," "medium close-up," and "voice-over" should be avoided. Remember, the person reading the document is not a media professional. The proposal and treatment are essentially sales tools designed to sell your ability to successfully complete your production within budget and on time, while accomplishing the stated objective.

The potential financial backers should be able to easily read and understand the proposal and treatment. They should be able to imagine exactly what the production will sound and look like without any other explanation or verbal description by the producer.

In reality, both the proposal and treatment may be written after the script has been finalized, because they must accurately reflect the script. From a practical point of view, the three preproduction writing functions may be prepared simultaneously.

Scene Script

The first completed draft of a script, the scene script, includes a detailed description of each scene and the action occurring during that scene, but not specific shots. Each scene description should indicate whether the scene is set during the day or at night and in an interior or exterior setting. The description should also describe the characters, key furniture/objects present, character movements, and all dialogue and narration.

Shooting Script

The shooting script is a more detailed version of the scene script. Each shot is described specifically and numbered in order. The framing—wide shot (WS), medium close-up (MCU), or close-up (CU)—is indicated, but the writer allows some leeway for the director's creativity. The descriptions should be complete enough that the director is able to interpret accurately what the writer had intended in each sequence, scene, or shot.

90

SAMPLE TREATMENT FORMAT

TITLE:	Safety Training	PAGE:	1
WRITER:	T. Bartlett	LENGTH: 10 mins	
CLIENT:	Mountain Industries	DATE: 10-10-04	

The ten-minute training tape will open with a montage of incorrect logging operations followed in each case by the possible disastrous and life-threatening results of such actions. Examples of such scenes are:

A logger without a safety belt steps back and falls from
a tree stand.

A chainsaw jams and flips back into the logger.

A tractor tips over on the driver because it exceeded its tilt
limit.

A logging truck driven too fast forces an oncoming car from the
road.

A log falls from a truck being loaded and strikes a logger who was
standing too close to the truck.

A logger refuels his saw improperly, causing a fire.

A truck or tractor becomes a runaway when left improperly
locked down.

A logger is dumped into the river and is crushed by logs.

A log avalanche occurs because of careless blocking of a log
stack.

This series of accidents will be enhanced with sound effects and dramatic music as well as the actual sound of each accident.

Following this montage, the narrator will walk into the scene and describe in general the dangers and reasons for following OSHA safety requirements for those working in dangerous occupations such as the

(continued)

Preproduction Planning II

Single-Column Script Format

Two basic script formats are used in preparing scripts for electronic field production (EFP): the traditional film single-column format and the traditional television dual-column format.

The single-column format evolved from stage script format to motion picture format to radio format before it was adapted again for video productions. The format defines various aspects of the scripts by varying the width of the margins and by capitalizing certain portions of the copy. The rules at first seem complex, but they can be summarized as follows:

- Each shot starts with the shot number at the extremes of the right- and left-hand margins. In uppercase type, either the word DAY or NIGHT indicates lighting conditions, followed by either INT or EXT, to indicate location.
- Camera directions, scene descriptions, and stage directions appear next, within slightly narrower margins. How the line is to be delivered is typed in still narrower margins within parentheses, and dialogue is typed within even narrower margins.
- The name of the speaking character is centered above his or her line in uppercase letters.
- Single-spacing is used for dialogue, camera angles and movements, stage directions, scene descriptions, sound effects, or cues.
- Double-spacing is used to separate a camera shot or scene from the next camera shot or scene, a scene from an interceding transition (FADE IN/FADE OUT, DISSOLVE), the speech of one character from the heading of the next character, and a speech from camera or stage directions.
- Uppercase type is used for interior (INT) or exterior (EXT) in heading line; indication of location; indication of day (DAY) or night (NIGHT); name of a character when first introduced in the stage directions and to indicate the character's dialogue; camera angles and movements; scene transitions; and indication of scene continuation (CONTINUED), if a scene is split between pages (avoid if at all possible).

MASTER SCENE SCRIPT FORMAT

(Margins and tabs set as indicated below. assuming 80 space wide paper)

| 5 | 10 | 20 | 25 | | 55 | 60 | | 70 | 75 |

FADE IN:

1.   INT/EXT   DAY/NIGHT   1.
BRIEF SCENE OR SHOT DESCRIPTION, CAM. ANGLE.

In upper and lower case, a more detailed description of the scene giving setting, props, and CHARACTERS position if needed with margins set at 10/70.

CHARACTER
(Mode of delivery, upper and
lower case, margins at 25/55)

The dialog is typed in upper and lower case
centered within 20/60 margins.

Any other descriptions of shot framing, movement of CAMERA or CHARACTER, are at margins set at 10/70.

(TRANSITION)

2.   INT   WS   UNIVERSITY CLASSROOM   DAY   2.

Classroom is full of students, some wide awake and gossiping, others sleeping or nodding off as they wait for the professor to arrive.

JANE
(Quietly so only Jack can hear her.)
Are you sure there isn't going to be an exam
during tomorrow's class?

JACK
(With a bravado, all-knowing tone)
Of course not, have I ever lied to you?

The professor enters the room, downstage right, walks to the lectern and the room becomes quiet.

PROFESSOR
(Emphatically as a reminder)
If I have no choice but to repeat myself again,
I WILL be forced to give you your first examination
in tomorrow's class.

(DISSOLVE TO)

3.   EXT   WS   CAMPUS   DAY   3.

The clouds suddenly darken the sky as rain, thunder and lightning start and the lights go out, plunging the room into darkness.

(A scene script describes the entire scene in very general terms. A shooting script contains much more detailed descriptions and shot instructions.)

Single-Column Script Format

Dual-Column Script Format

The dual-column television script format evolved from the audiovisual and instructional film formats. It is based on separating audio instructions and information from visual instructions. Two columns are set up on the page. The video instructions are located on the left side of the page, and the audio instructions are on the right side. This is not an absolute rule; some operations prefer the opposite, and some include a storyboard on the left, right, or down the middle of the page.

Each shot number is identified in both the video and audio columns, matching the appropriate audio with its video counterpart. All video and audio instructions are typed in uppercase letters. Copy to be read by the performers is typed in uppercase and lowercase letters. Many performers, especially news anchors, prefer all uppercase letters in the misguided belief that uppercase copy is easier to read. However, all readability studies indicate the opposite, and most computerized prompter systems currently display copy in both uppercase and lowercase letters.

Video instructions are arranged in single-spaced blocks, whereas audio copy is presented in double-spaced blocks. Triple-spacing between shots helps both the talent and the director follow the flow of the script. The name of the talent is typed in uppercase letters to the left of the right-hand column. If the same audio source continues through several shots, it is not necessary to repeat the source's name unless another source intervenes.

Avoid hyphenating words at the end of a line and avoid splitting shots at the bottom of the page. Spreading copy out allows for notes and additional instructions to be added during actual production.

Information concerning the production should be repeated at the top of each page—for example, the title, writer's name, and other pertinent information. Each page must be numbered in sequence. If pages are added, letters or other indications may be added to keep the pages in order (for example, page 25a falls between pages 25 and 26).

Computer programs have been designed to facilitate the preparation of scripts by allowing the writer to concentrate on the creative part of writing rather than the formatting. These computer applications are specifically designed for both single- and double-column scripts in a variety of formats, including television, audio/video, multimedia, motion pictures, and radio.

DUAL-COLUMN SCRIPT FORMAT

TITLE: PAGE:
WRITER: LENGTH:
CLIENT: DATE:

VIDEO	AUDIO
1. SINGLE-SPACE VIDEO INSTRUCTIONS	1. ANNCR: Audio copy is lined up directly across the page from its matching video.
2. TRIPLE-SPACE BETWEEN EACH SHOT	2. Double-space between each line of audio copy.
3. EACH SHOT MUST BE NUMBERED ON THE SCRIPT	3. The audio column's number must match that of its video.
4. EVERYTHING THE VIEWER IS TO SEE; ALL VISUALS, VIDEO TAPES, CG, CAMERA SHOTS, ARE INCLUDED IN THE LEFT-HAND COLUMN.	4. Everything the viewer is to hear; all sounds, music, voices, sound effects, narration and all audio cues are included in the right-hand column.
5. EVERYTHING ON THE VIDEO SIDE IS TYPED IN CAPITAL LETTERS.	5. Everything spoken by the talent is typed in upper and lower case letters. All instructions in the audio column are typed in capital letters.
6. THE TALENT'S NAME STARTS EACH NEW LINE, BUT DOES NOT HAVE TO BE REPEATED IF THE SAME PERSON OR SOUND SOURCE CONTINUES.	6. SAM: Note--the name is in caps, what Sam says is in upper and lower case.
7. AVOID SPLITTING SHOTS AT BOTTOM OF THE PAGE.	7. Avoid splitting words or thoughts at the end of the line.

Dual-Column Script Format

Storyboards

Storyboards are paper visualizations of the production. They provide a flexible means of working out sequences, framing, and shot relationships before bringing an expensive cast and crew together for the actual production. Storyboards are usually organized in three parts: picture, copy/instructions, and shot number.

Generally, a storyboard form displays a 4 : 3 or 16 : 9 area, with rounded corners, that contains the video frame, with a small space above the frame for writing in the shot number. Below the frame is an area, usually slightly smaller than the frame, designed to contain the audio and/or other specific instructions for that shot. Storyboard forms are available in preprinted packets or as a computer program template. Such templates allow the writer/artist to draw and redraw until the design is satisfactory without creating stacks of printed boards. Such templates may be passed among creative staff for alterations and feedback before the final script is created.

The key objects in the shot are sketched into the frame block. These visual representations can be as simple as stick figures or as accurate as color photographs. The more accurate the drawings, the more serviceable the storyboard will be in solving problems during preproduction and production. The matching space for instructions may contain "pan," "dolly," or other camera movement or composition concepts. The shot number must match the shot number on the script. If additions or deletions are made, then the shot number changes must be made to both the script and the storyboard. Each shot should be represented by at least one storyboard frame. In some cases, additional frames may be necessary to show beginning and ending frame positions if a pan, dolly, or zoom is indicated.

Once completed, storyboard frames can be placed on a wall or flannel board so that they can be rearranged easily. Standing back and looking at all of the storyboard frames gives the director, writer, and producer a better overall view of the production and can provide a way to spot problem areas or solutions to problems.

Because the storyboard frame, description, and shot number can be separated from other storyboard frames, their order can be manipulated until the best possible shot sequence is reached. This process may prevent continuity problems by avoiding jump cuts and may create a more organized method of shooting the production.

Once the complete storyboard order has been arranged, the final shooting script can be written.

STORYBOARDS

Super Title over Logo
V.O. Announcer

EST Shot of Dome
Music Up

MS Host
Host: "Hello, I'm Dave Smith..."

Location Scouting

A notion of the type of shooting location required should be determined early on in the production conceptualization process. Specific locations can be chosen after the scene script has been written, but the location must be finalized before the shooting script has been completed.

In addition to the obvious characteristics to look for in a location—accessibility and having the right setting or appearance—there are some factors that are less obvious. A location that can be used without cost, such as near parking, power, and sanitary facilities, and that is convenient to storage space for equipment and materials is worth the search. Access to temperature-controlled areas for cast and crew to use between takes is also important. Once a location has been chosen, arrange a meeting with the site authority.

At this meeting, the following information must be collected: names, phone numbers, and exact location or addresses of authorities who control the areas and locations to be used. These individuals may be the resident, building engineer, building manager, janitor, department head, or a civil employee in charge of public areas. Make certain that the person who has given permission to use the location actually has the authority to do so and then get permission in writing with a location release.

While meeting with the site authority, the producer should explain fully how the site will be used, what changes may be necessary, how restoration will be handled, and what access the production crew will need to the location. Discuss every possible contingency that could occur during the production process to avoid any unresolved differences during actual production.

Put into writing all agreements, have the site authority sign them, keep copies, give the site authority copies, and send copies to the ultimate authority of the location. This should be done well before the shoot is scheduled so that any problems can be resolved before the cast and crew arrive for the shoot.

MOUNTAIN PRODUCTIONS
LOCATION RELEASE

I hereby irrevocably grant to _Mountain Productions_ the right to use the property described below which is owned and/or controlled by me at _____
(full legal description of property)
in connection with the production, duplication, and/or distribution of the video, film, or sound recording program, segment, or shots recorded on:
_____, by Mountain Productions.
(Date)

I hereby assign to Mountain Productions all rights, title, and interest in the materials as they are integrated into the final master film, videotape, or audio recording, granting full and unrestricted permission and authority to Mountain Productions to record, reproduce, and use in any manner, media, or form whatsoever including securing copyrights for the final master and subsequent copies of all media materials produced which includes the image of my property, warranting that I have unrestricted right to make this grant and assignment and hereby release and agree to indemnify and save harmless Mountain Productions , its staff and agents for any and all liability, claims, actions, and damages arising in a manner from the material which contains the image of my property.

For the use of the above described property and the right described in this clearance, Mountain Productions agrees to compensate me as follows: _____.

I express my intention to be firmly and legally bound this

_____ day of _____, 20____ .

_____   _____
(Signature)   (Witness)

_____   _____
(Print Name)   (Print Name)

_____   _____
(Street Address)   (Street Address)

_____   _____
(City-State-Zip)   (City-State-Zip)

Location Scouting

99

Site Survey and Location Planning

Be sure to visit the location at the time of day, day of the week, and, if possible, day of the month that the production will be shot. This precautionary act may help avoid hindrances such as unplanned traffic and noise, lighting, and ambient sound problems. Each room or space to be used should be measured accurately, and a scale drawing should be plotted indicating the locations and sizes of windows and doors and placement of furniture, walls, and power sources. In addition to the location of power outlets, the location of the fuse or circuit breaker box should be determined. Discuss with the site authority whether you may tap into the fuse box or if it can be left open in case a fuse or breaker blows. If the box is left open, the crew can correct problems without waiting for the box to be unlocked or handled by an assigned person. While checking the location of the fuse box, check the power rating of each circuit and determine which circuits control specific outlets that may be used for the shoot.

After all of the measurements have been taken and the plot is drawn, then possible locations for performers and cameras should be identified. Note the movements of the performers, as well as camera movements. If furniture needs to be moved or extra furniture or set pieces are required, this should be indicated on the plot. The plot is a scale diagram drawn as if you are looking straight down on the location. It is not drawn in perspective and is useless if not drawn to an accurate scale.

Before leaving the site meeting, determine from the site authority where production vehicles may be safely and legally parked and the location of a loading area. When possible, choose a loading/parking location that is well lit and has some security. If the location does not provide security for vehicles, it may be necessary to hire or provide your own security personnel. If permits for parking and/or loading are required, determine the process and authority for obtaining such permits. Keep in mind that not even public property can be used for any production purpose without permission, a permit, and often a fee.

Before leaving the site during the survey, recheck all of the information gathered and make certain that you have all the necessary facts, permits, measurements, and telephone numbers. Make sure that there are no conflicts or contradictions in your lists.

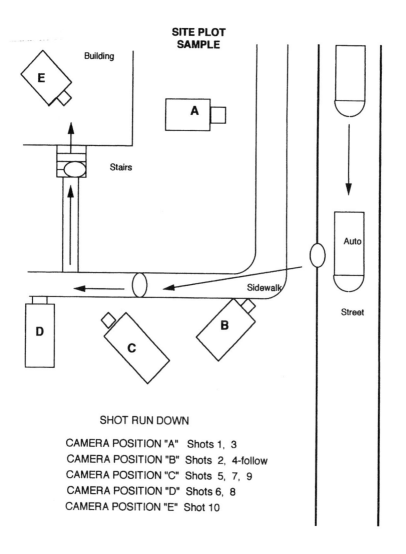

SITE PLOT SAMPLE

Building

E

A

Stairs

Auto

Street

Sidewalk

D

C

B

SHOT RUN DOWN

CAMERA POSITION "A"   Shots 1, 3
CAMERA POSITION "B"   Shots 2, 4-follow
CAMERA POSITION "C"   Shots 5, 7, 9
CAMERA POSITION "D"   Shots 6, 8
CAMERA POSITION "E"   Shot 10

Site Survey and Location Planning

Organizing Equipment

Once the site survey has been completed, the director, camera operator, gaffer, and audio operator meet to list the equipment required for the shoot. If possible, these three key crew members should accompany the director on the site survey. Each crew chief is responsible for the equipment needed to fulfill his or her responsibilities, but a production meeting should be held to double-check all aspects of the production and to provide an opportunity for an exchange of ideas, solutions to problems, and resolutions to unanswered concerns.

Making a list of equipment helps ensure that everything has been thought of that will be needed. It can also be used as a checklist when packing up the equipment to make certain that nothing has been left behind at the end of the shoot. The director confers with the crew chiefs on the skills and number of crew members required. Most EFP shoots are organized with the intention of using a minimum number of people, but the complexity of the production determines the size of the crew.

Once all the lists are completed, the director and producer work out a detailed schedule that starts with that day and ends with the delivery of the finished product. Each stage of the production should be organized on a *timeline* designed so that each stage can proceed independently, and therefore will be unaffected by delays in other stages. However, the interdependency of media production also makes a timeline critical in the efficient completion of any project.

With the completed shooting script and plot in hand, the director can sit down at the site later and determine which shots are to be made from each camera location. The director should indicate on a *shooting list* (shot sheet) which shots are to be shot at each camera location and the order in which they are to be shot. The most efficient use of cast, crew, and equipment should be the key factor in this determination. Make certain that all possible shots are planned from each location before the camera and lights are moved to the next location.

TIMELINE PLOT

DATE	RESEARCH WRITING	PREPROD. SURVEYS	PRODUCTION	POSTPROD.
Jan. 1	Begin research			
Jan. 15	Develop concept			
Feb. 1	Deliver proposal			
Feb. 15	Deliver treatment			
March 1	Complete research			
March 15	Treatment approved			
April 1		Location scouting		
April 15	Scene script approved	Sign location contracts		
May 1	Shooting script approved	Cast-crew equipment contracts		
May 15		Begin rehearsals	Set up for shooting	
June 1				Begin editing
June 15			Complete major videography	
July 30			Pick-up shots	Review rough cut
Aug. 1				
Aug. 15				Deliver answer print
Aug. 30				Deliver completed master

The Production Process: Production

Production Stages and Setup

In the production process, there are four standard stages in the actual shooting of an electronic field production (EFP): setting up, rehearsing, shooting, and striking.

Setting Up

Assuming all of the preproduction steps were followed, the first step of the production stage is unloading the equipment and moving it to the first shooting location. Regarding security, professional video equipment is expensive and looks attractive to thieves. Never leave equipment unguarded and never leave the production vehicle unlocked.

Field Equipment Considerations

Field equipment is much more susceptible than studio equipment to damage and technical problems from the environment. Because the majority of the operating parts are electronic, at a certain level of humidity, the equipment becomes inoperative. This is particularly true of tape decks. In addition, keep all liquids away from electronic equipment. Severely cold weather slows parts of mechanical equipment, such as the motors that drive decks and zoom lenses. Extreme heat affects circuits inside the camera and decks and may damage tape stock. In most cases, these factors can be compensated for, but they must be taken into consideration when planning a field production. If the camera records directly onto a computer hard disk, memory card, or disc medium, the same considerations need to be taken to prevent moisture, dust, or both from entering the medium case. If the signal is recorded onto a chip, that process does not require any moving mechanical operations, making the camcorder much more rugged and impervious to temperature and humidity changes.

Camera

Once the camera's position is set, the tripod is set up. Its legs need to be set in a wide enough stance to provide a stable base, but not spread so far apart that they are in the way of traffic or the operator. The tripod's height should be adjusted to the eye level of the subject, unless the director requires a special angle.

Level the head of the tripod with the bubble level, and then mount the camera on the head. Make certain the pan and tilt locks are tight; if the tripod head does not have locks, tighten the drag controls so that the camera will not tilt out of control. Set the drag controls tight enough that there is enough back pressure to allow for a smooth, even pan or tilt, but not so tight as to cause a jerk when you try to pan or tilt.

SETTING UP EQUIPMENT

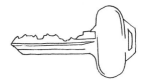

ALWAYS lock the vehicle when leaving expensive equipment unattended.

Use a cart to move heavy equipment.

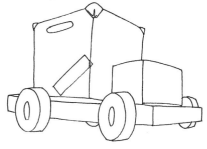

After determining the camera position, set up the tripod.

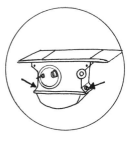

The tripod head should be "bubble-leveled," and the pan and tilt locks should be tightened.

Production Stages and Setup

Lighting Preparation

As soon as the crew arrives at the location, the lighting director or gaffer should run the power cable to the camcorder or recorder and then string power cables to the lighting instrument locations. After the camera is in position, the gaffer can start placing the instruments. Power cables should be run where there is the least amount of foot traffic and out of sight of the camera, yet with as short a run as possible.

Proper lighting is an artistic endeavor. Although there is much science and practicality to lighting design, it is probably the most artistic portion of video production. There are no hard and fast rules, only guidelines. There are typical and traditional setups, but every lighting situation is unique and must be approached from an individualistic direction. The lighting depends partly on the director and writer's concept of the production and partly on the requirements set by the location, budget, equipment, and amount of time allotted to create the desired lighting ambiance.

Three types of lighting are basic for EFP productions: *realistic, abstract,* and *neutral.* Dramatic productions and some types of commercials require as realistic a lighting setting as possible. Music videos, some commercials, and science fiction dramas may require abstract lighting that goes beyond realism. Neutral lighting is often used for game shows, some newscasts, situation comedies, and some commercials. Hard and fast rules defining each of these types of lighting do not exist, but the end result must match the director's requirements.

Lighting for high-definition (HD) production requires greater attention to detail and the functions of highly critical cameras. It is not a matter of more light but rather a better placement of lighting instruments and the shadows and light patterns that follow. Because the better HD cameras can handle a broader range of contrast ratios, a matching wider range of effects may be obtained with lighting that is more difficult to achieve in standard definition (SD) production.

In addition to the director's requirements for the lighting—that is, that it set the mood, time, and type of production—the lighting must provide enough base illumination for the camera to create a usable image. As discussed previously under "Lighting Instruments," the camera or chips reproduce what is presented to them. The light must be of the correct color and intensity and within the contrast range of the particular type of camera in use. These three factors—color, intensity, and contrast—control the basic lighting setup. Once they have been satisfied, creative and innovative lighting techniques may be used.

TYPES OF LIGHTING

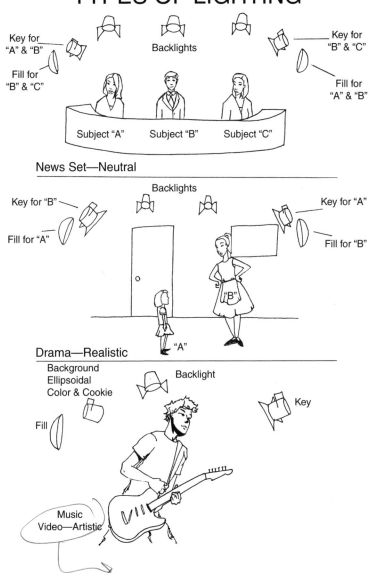

Key for "A" & "B"

Fill for "B" & "C"

Backlights

Key for "B" & "C"

Fill for "A" & "B"

Subject "A"   Subject "B"   Subject "C"

News Set—Neutral

Key for "B"

Fill for "A"

Backlights

Key for "A"

Fill for "B"

"B"

"A"

Drama—Realistic

Background
Ellipsoidal
Color & Cookie

Backlight

Key

Fill

Music
Video—Artistic

109

Controlling Color Temperature

Studio productions control color temperature by installing lamps with the same color temperature output in all lighting fixtures. In the field, controlling color temperature is not this simple. Windows, fluorescent lighting fixtures, and even standard incandescent fixtures create a variation in color temperature, even though all of the instruments may be lamped with the same Kelvin temperature bulbs. If possible, light a set only with lighting instruments lamped with the proper bulbs. Windows should be covered with drapes, blinds, or a large sheet of Wratten 85 (yellow–orange) filter material. This accomplishes two tasks. First, it changes the daylight entering the window, resulting in an effect similar to light produced by 3,200 K lamps. Second, it cuts the intensity of the bright daylight by one or two stops.

Another method of lighting with daylight entering a room is to convert the field lighting fixtures to approximate daylight by covering them with Wratten 82 (blue) filter material or a dichroic filter. This helps match the mixed lighting, but it does not help balance the difference in light intensity between the daylight and the lighting instruments. This is because the blue filter reduces the lighting instrument output by about half, requiring more powerful or a greater number of lamps.

If many incandescent fixtures are present and cannot be covered or turned off, the white balance circuits of most video cameras will reach white balance without a filter in place. A pale blue filter may be necessary to reach truer white.

When shooting in a location lit by existing office fluorescent lamps, there are several possible solutions. First, the process used to white balance when only fluorescent lamps are present is determined by the type of fluorescent tube. Newer tubes designed specifically for media production are designed to match either daylight or tungsten lighting Kelvin temperature. If these tubes are not available, a daylight (85) filter in the camera can bring the color close to normal. This reduces the light input, but not radically. If white balance cannot be reached, the tubes may be covered with a light magenta filter or specially manufactured filters that slip over the fluorescent tubes. Because fluorescent lights give off a nearly shadowless fill light, it is also possible to light a scene with fairly bright professional tungsten lamps as key lights and thus overpower the fluorescent fixtures. This is another example of mixed lighting. New portable fluorescent and liquid crystal display (LCD) lighting fixtures balanced close to daylight, which provide another method of field flat lighting, are currently available.

COMPENSATING LENS FILTERS

Neutral Density

Light loss	Filter
1/3 stop	.10
2/3 stop	.20
1 stop	.30
1-1/3 stops	.40
1-2/3 stops	.50
2 stops	.60
3 stops	.90

Color Correction

Conversion in Units Kelvin	Light loss	Filter
3200 to 5400	2 stops	80A
5400 to 3200	2/3 stops	85B
3000 to 3200	1/3 stops	82A

Fluorescent Correction

Light loss	Filter
1/3 stop	CC-05M
2/3 stop	CC-30M

The total light loss with a combination of filters is the sum of the individual losses.

Controlling Light Intensity

In a studio setting, the intensity of light is controlled in a variety of ways: by varying the voltage to each instrument through a dimmer board, by adding *filters* or *scrims* to the instruments, or by mounting or moving instruments closer or farther away from the subject.

In the field, light intensity controls are limited by the types of portable equipment available. These limitations are determined by the size and budget of the production. For the average EFP production, simpler means of light control than those used in the studio are necessary.

Generally, the lighting instruments used in the field are open-faced instruments; that is, the light is harsher and more difficult to control. Using scrims and filters and bouncing the light softens, diffuses, and reduces the light level to that required for fill lights. Key light levels and backlight levels may also be controlled by using scrims and filters.

Small, portable dimmers are available for field use, but decreasing the voltage of a tungsten lamp changes the color temperature approximately 100 degrees for each 10-volt variation. Portable dimmers tend to be heavy and bulky and often require an electrician to hook them up to a breaker box to obtain the necessary power.

The most practical way to control light intensity in the field is the placement of the lighting instruments. Because light levels follow the inverse square law, a relatively small movement of a lamp makes a major difference in the light level falling on the subject. If a lamp provides 100-foot candles of light at a distance of 10 feet from the subject, moving the lamp to 5 feet boosts the light level to 400-foot candles (the inverse square of ½ equals 4 times the original light level; therefore, 100 becomes 400). If the lamp is moved back to 20 feet, the light level decreases to 25-foot candles (the inverse square of 2 equals ¼ times the original light level of 100, resulting in 25-foot candles).

Most EFP lighting directors can achieve the light levels and effects required by the director with a combination of lighting instrument placement and the judicious use of scrims, filters, barn doors, and flags.

112

LAMP ACCESSORIES

Scrim   Half Scrim   Cookie

INVERSE SQUARE LAW

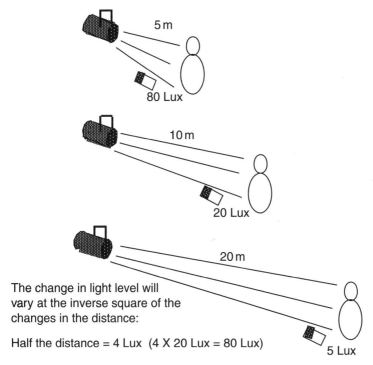

5 m

80 Lux

10 m

20 Lux

20 m

The change in light level will vary at the inverse square of the changes in the distance:

Half the distance = 4 Lux (4 X 20 Lux = 80 Lux)

5 Lux

Double the distance = 1/4 Lux (1/4 of 20 Lux = 5 Lux)

Controlling Light Intensity

Contrast Range

The control for contrast is a little more complex. A reflected spotlight meter is needed to measure the amount of light reflected from the brightest and the darkest objects in the picture. These light measurements are called *reflectance values*. The tricky part of taking these measurements is that if there are either highly reflective or very dark objects in the frame, these should be excluded from the reading. A judgment must be made as to whether it is necessary to reproduce detail in either of those areas. If the amount of light reflected from the brightest portion of the frame in which detail is required is more than 30 to 40 times the light in the darkest area needed for detail, then additional full light is needed on the dark areas or some light needs to be taken off the lighter areas. By carefully lighting for the contrast range of the video camera, you can avoid important areas "blooming" or "flaring" into a white mass or large areas appearing so dark and black that they look "muddy." The newest digital cameras equipped with the latest chips can handle a greater contrast range of up to 40 : 1, compared with 30 : 1 in cameras with older chips.

The most difficult situations for maintaining proper contrast range are those shot in the bright sunlight or at night with available light. During a cloudless, bright day, it is nearly impossible to balance the bright sun with any other light source to maintain contrast range. The best method for balancing the lighting is to use the sun as the backlight and reflect the sunlight back toward the subject.

Night lighting is more difficult. Some source of fill is needed to overcome the bright, harsh light from streetlights, automobile headlights, advertising signs, and other lights. The easiest method is to shoot at dawn or dusk, except that the period when there is enough light to shoot and still have it look like night is very short. Another method is to shoot day for night. This involves white balancing with a yellow rather than a white board and underexposing by two stops or using an 82 (dark blue) filter and underexposing by two stops. In day-for-night shots, streetlights, auto lights, and other light sources that are normally on at night must be turned on, even though the scene is actually being shot during the day.

CONTRAST RANGE

Light Source

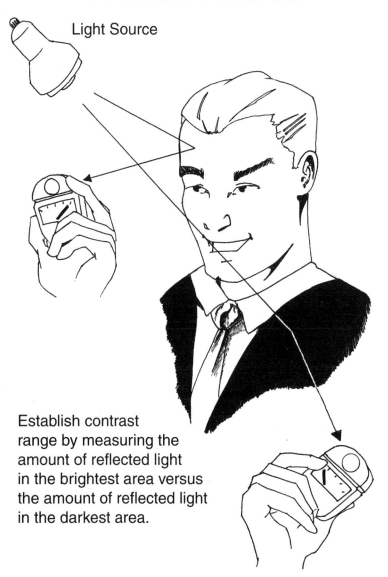

Establish contrast range by measuring the amount of reflected light in the brightest area versus the amount of reflected light in the darkest area.

Basic Three-Point Lighting

Lighting practice is based on two suppositions: that there will be enough light for the camera to create a reasonably useful picture and that the appearance will fulfill the look that the director desires. *Basic three-point* lighting is designed to satisfy both of these requirements. Three-point lighting derives its name from the three lighting instruments used to achieve satisfactory levels and appearance: key lights, fill lights, and backlights. The *key light* duplicates the major light source in our lives—the sun; secondarily, it duplicates the overhead lighting present in most homes and workspaces. The *fill light* balances the key light, reducing the contrast ratio and softening the harsh look of a one-light source. The *backlight* adds a rim of light around the subject to separate it from the background and adds a third dimension to the two-dimensional video field.

Backlight

The backlight is usually the first instrument set in place, because once performers, set pieces, and props are in place, it is difficult to reach the proper position for a backlight. The next light to be set is the key light; then the fill, kickers, set, and extra lights are set. The backlight instrument is mounted above and slightly behind the major subject and directly opposite the camera position. Because this lamp is focused toward the camera, it is necessary to use barn doors or a flag to avoid having the backlight shine directly into the lens of the camera.

Key Light

The key light is the main source of light. It should always have motivation; that is, there should be a reason for its angle and position. If there is no apparent motivation, then set the key about 45 degrees above the camera and from 60 to 40 degrees to one side of the camera. The key should be the brightest light under normal circumstances. It can create shadows, adding depth to the picture, and should set the major color temperature for that shot or scene.

Fill Light

The fill light represents the reflected light from clouds, the sky, buildings, and multiple light sources found in buildings. In some ways, it is, like the backlight, an artificial light, but it is important in video production to bring the contrast ratio down to a level that a video camera can handle. The fill light should be mounted on the opposite side of the camera from the key, should be of a lower intensity, should be softer and more diffused, and should not create any visible shadows.

Fixed Single Subject

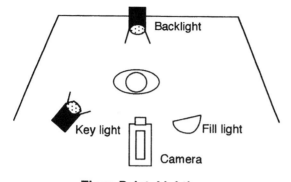

Three-Point Lighting

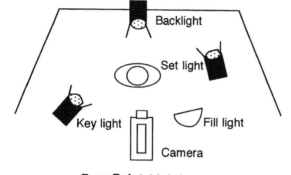

Four-Point Lighting

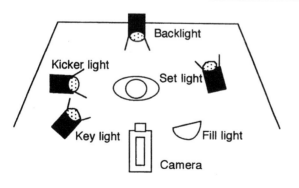

Five-Point Lighting

More Complex Lighting

Kicker and Set Lights

A variety of other lighting instruments may be needed to create either realistic light or the effect desired in the scene. The two most common instruments are the kicker and the set light.

The *kicker* is a light mounted to one side of the subject so that it throws its light along the side of the subject. This light functions much like the backlight by helping separate the subject from the background, thus adding depth to the frame.

The *set light* is designed to highlight specific areas of the set. Sometimes it also separates the subject from the set, but more often it is designed to draw attention to particular areas of the set, such as a logo, an important set piece, or a lit area of an otherwise dark background.

Multiple and/or Moving Subjects

Lighting a single subject that does not move during the recording is relatively simple. The lighting process becomes complicated when there is more than one subject in the frame and those subjects begin to move about on camera.

Multiple subjects may be lit by spreading the light wider to take in more than one subject, but this method is usually unsatisfactory. Unless both subjects are facing the same direction and are an equal distance from the light source, they will be lit unevenly.

One solution is to *cross-key* light; that is, use the key light for the subject on one side as the fill for the subject on the other side and vice versa. Working with more than two subjects may require key lights for each subject and a widespread series of fill lights covering the entire area. The major problem with multiple key lights is the possibility that the lights will create multiple shadows. The multiple shadows may be avoided by washing out some of the shadows with fill and set lights or by focusing the keys so that the shadows fall outside of the area covered by the camera frame.

If subjects move, lighting becomes even more complex. One solution is to arrange key lights and backlights so that they throw a relatively even pattern of light over the area of movement at an equal distance from the light source. Fill is easily flooded out to cover the entire area. Another solution is to break the movement down into several shots. Each shot will cover only a small portion of the movement area and can be more easily lit because the subject can be lit in roughly the same intensity for each shot.

COMPLEX LIGHTING PLOTS

Multiple Subjects

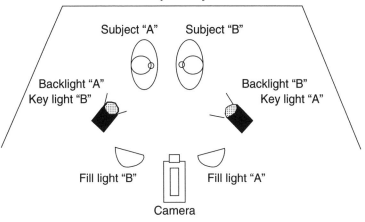

Moving Subject(s)

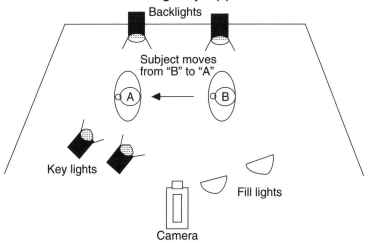

Multiple lighting sources need to be set
without creating multiple shadows.

119

Creative Lighting

Beyond providing enough light for the camera to produce a usable picture, lighting is also a key creative visual element. It sets the mood and may be used to indicate the time, the date, and the location of a production.

Mood Lighting

From the first moment an audience sees the opening shots of a situation comedy, they are made aware that they are in for some lighthearted entertainment. Much of that realization comes from the high-key, low-contrast, nearly shadowless lighting used, known as *Notan* lighting. This term originated from Japanese artists who painted brightly lit scenes without any shadows. The brightly lit set without any dark areas lets the audience know the mood the director wants them to experience.

On the other hand, should the first shot of a scene be lit with low-key, high-contrast, heavy, dark shadows, the audience is made aware that a heavy drama follows. This type of lighting is called *chiaroscuro;* this term is borrowed from the Italian painters who used the same high contrast to set the mood of their paintings. The lighting (in addition to the set, costumes, coloring, and mannerisms of the actors) gives the audience the advance information that they probably will not spend much time laughing during this scene. Of course, all creative techniques may be used in contrast; a comedy scene may be lit in low key to make it funnier because it is unexpected.

Lighting for Time, Date, and Location

Using lighting to indicate time, date, and location is subtle but should always be taken into consideration when designing a scene. Early morning and late afternoon light is different from that at high noon. The colors are different (light is warmer/redder early and late in the day), and the angle of the light is lower. Winter sun is bluer and colder; the lights of summer, fall, and spring each have their own colors and contrast levels. A setting in the tropics has a higher key light than that of a northern European city or a slum setting.

Light may also be used simply as an abstract creative object in and of itself. Light slashes across the background provide a feeling of prison bars, window slats, venetian blinds, or other setting not actually present. Cukaloris patterns on a plain background tell the audience an infinite number of characteristics about a scene. A cukaloris is a metal disc inserted into an ellipsoidal spotlight that creates a light pattern or mottled design on the background. Each location should be carefully analyzed for the proper light level, angle, color, and contrast settings to fit the intended mood desired by the director.

120

ELLIPSOIDAL SPOT and CUKALORIS (Cookie) PATTERNS

Without a pattern

With a pattern

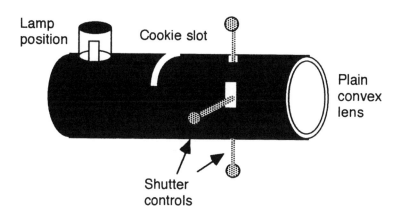

Lamp position

Cookie slot

Plain convex lens

Shutter controls

Sets and Properties

For most field productions, sets and properties (props) exist at the chosen location. The convenience of using already existing rooms, furniture, and other props may be one of the main reasons for shooting a production in the field. At the same time, the careful choice of a location is critical in the field production process.

There are three levels of items in this category: sets, set pieces, and hand props. *Sets* are backgrounds. They may be actual walls, trees, construction made of cloth or wood, or simply the actual location suitable for the particular production. *Set pieces* are items attached to or placed within a set. Generally, set pieces include paintings on walls, furniture, automobiles, or bookcases. *Hand props* are items small enough to be picked up and handled, but for the most part, they are items that need to be handled by the talent during the production.

Choices in each of the categories are made by the director and art director. They should match the tone, time period, quality, and attitude of the production. A beautiful painting should not hang in a set that is supposed to be a dingy office. At the same time, a cheap, poorly done painting should not be seen in a room designed to be the office of a Fortune 500 chief executive office (CEO). These choices must be made from knowledge of art, architecture, and interior design.

Designing for HD is much more critical than designing (and execution of design) for SD. The increased detail of HD shows every small defect in appearance; every sloppy paint job; and every poorly matched, worn, or outdated set pieces. Design for HD must be examined with a magnifying glass to check each and every detail in the completed design before cameras start rolling.

As in lighting design, set design sends a clearly defined message to the audience and must match the rest of the production to avoid confusing and misleading the audience. Set design decisions should be made during preproduction planning, but often they cannot be made until the setup period with the crew on location. Rearranging furniture, rehanging paintings, and removing unnecessary or conflicting items from a room being used as a location site should be accomplished during the setup period.

SET DRESSINGS

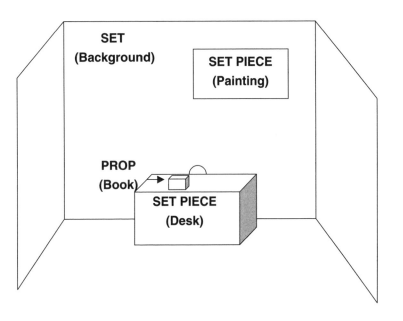

SETS are background and walls
SET PIECES are furniture and decorative items
PROPS are items handled by performers

Setting Up the Audio

While the camera operator and gaffer are setting up their equipment, the audio operator strings mic cables or sets up the receivers for wireless mics. If a mixer is used, the cables are strung to the mixer and the output of the mixer to the recorder or camcorder. Levels are checked to ensure that the entire audio system is operating and is balanced.

If a boom mic is used, its position needs to be checked with the camera operator, lighting director, and director. If body mics are used, the operator needs to place them on the talent, show the talent how to turn them on, and check that a signal at the proper level is being received at the mixer or recorder.

If playback audio is required, the audio operator must set up the speakers, cables, and audio source, such as a tape deck or compact disc (CD) player. If the production involves live music, then the audio operator has the responsibility of miking the band, soloists, or other music sources. In some cases, the director will require that the audio be recorded on a separate recorder. This arrangement is also the audio operator's responsibility.

Prompting

Often, some type of prompting device is needed, especially for commercial shoots. There are three basic types of prompters: handheld, camera-mounted, and in-ear devices.

Handheld prompters are pieces of poster board bearing either the entire copy lettered in large bold type or an outline of keywords around which the performer ad-libs.

The most common prompting device currently used is a monitor mounted above or below the camera lens with two angled mirrors reflecting the monitor image directly in front of the camera lens. This gives the audience the impression that the talent is looking directly at them, but in reality, the performer is looking at the image of the copy reflected from a mirror mounted in front of the camera lens. The source of the copy can be scripts that are taped together in a continuous sheet and passed under a black-and-white camera or scripts produced from a dedicated prompter computer or character generator.

The third method requires a special skill on the part of the talent. A small headset is placed in the ear of the talent, and a recording of the copy, previously made by the talent, is played back through the headset. Skilled announcers can repeat vast amounts of their own words slightly delayed from the original as if they were speaking from memory. Of course, the best option is to have a performer who has taken the time and trouble to memorize all of his or her lines.

PROMPTING DEVICES

Welcome back
to our show.
Today's guest is
Doctor Jean Smith...

Idiot Cards

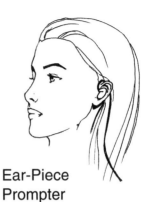

Ear-Piece
Prompter

Camera-Mounted Prompter

Rehearsing and Preparing Talent

While the crew is setting up the equipment, the director works with the talent and supervises all of the other operations. The director also checks on all sets, props, prompting devices, and other materials to be used in the first sequence. The setup period blends into the rehearsal period, but actual rehearsal cannot take place until cameras, lights, and mics are in place and the crew has received preliminary production instructions. Those instructions should include a written sheet for each crew member or crew section. The lighting director and key grip receive the instructions if a full crew is used; the gaffer and grip receive the instructions if there is one crew member for each position.

For the lighting and stage crew, a plot shows the position of the camera for each setup, talent positions and movements, key furniture, and backgrounds or other set pieces. The camera operator receives a shot sheet, which lists the camera positions in the order of setup and the shots to be completed at each camera position in the order they will be shot. A plot also is helpful for the camera operator.

During setup, the director makes certain that all talent are present, in makeup and costume, and prepared to shoot their scenes. General discussions may be carried on about relationships between actors and other objects while the crew is completing the setup process.

Once the location is ready, the director walks the actors through their starting locations, blocking, and movements, if there are any. The director has the camera operator watch the blocking rehearsal so that he or she can visualize the camera movements needed for each shot. At this time, the talent should deliver their lines with their mics properly placed so that the audio operator can set levels.

The director plays the role of benevolent dictator to the cast and crew. The director must have absolute control but must also respect and listen to the members of the crew for the benefit of their knowledge and expertise. No crew or cast member should argue with the director; however, a professional difference of opinion leading to a discussion is permissible if time permits. At the end of the discussion, the director's decision is final. The director's decision should be based on his or her knowledge of the entire production, not on the relatively narrow view held by each individual cast and crew member.

After a walk-through rehearsal has been successfully completed, several camera rehearsals should be run. This involves everyone on the cast and crew completing their roles as if the shot is being taped. Once the director is satisfied with the performances of both cast and crew, he or she orders a take to be shot.

126

LIGHTING PLOT AND SHOT RUNDOWN

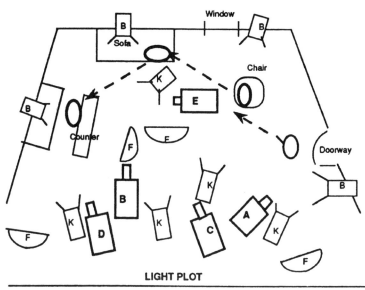

LIGHT PLOT

Shot Rundown	Plot Key
	Camera
Camera "A" Shots 1, 12	
Camera "B" Shots 3, 5, 7, 9	Key light
Camera "C" Shots 4, 6, 8	
Camera "D" Shots 10, 14	Fill Light
Camera "E" Shot 11	
	Backlight
	Talent

127

Shooting a Scene

The actual process for shooting a take is as follows: The director calls for quiet on the set by calling out "Quiet" or "Stand by." At that command, complete silence is expected from all cast and crew members. If the shoot is at a public location, a crew member may have to circulate through the adjacent crowd and quiet the crowd, unless the noise of the crowd is part of the audio ambiance. At the "Stand by" cue, all cast and crew assume their starting positions and prepare physically and mentally for the beginning of the shot.

When the director believes everyone is ready, he or she calls "Roll tape," "Roll it," or maybe even "Roll 'em." As soon as the tape deck is up to speed, either the camera operator, if a camcorder is used, or the tape operator, if a separate recorder is being used, calls out "Speed," or "Locked in," or "Framed." The director performs a 5-second count, either silently or out loud, and then calls "Action." This 5-second delay is necessary to ensure that the tape deck has recorded at least 5 seconds of clean synchronization (sync) and control track or time code, which is needed for editing purposes. Professional actors will pause for a beat and then start their movement or lines. The crew will follow the action as directed during rehearsals.

During a take, there are three people who may shout "Cut." The major responsibility lies with the director, but the camera operator and the audio operator also may cut a shot. If the camera operator sees in the viewfinder a visual error bad enough to make the take unusable, he or she may yell "Cut." It is best to quickly consult with the director before cutting a shot in the event that the audio portion of the take is usable, even though the video portion is not. The audio operator has the same responsibility in monitoring the recorded audio. If a noise is present that causes the take to be unusable, the audio operator may call "Cut"; again, because there is always a chance that the video portion is usable, the audio operator rarely cuts a take without a quick conference with the director. Also, an audio operator seldom cuts a take because, if necessary, most audio can be looped or rerecorded in a Foley session during postproduction. Any crew member may shout "Cut" if a situation occurs that may hurt a cast or crew member. A *Foley session* is a special postproduction sound effects session during which all of the various ambient and replacement sounds are created to match the action of the production.

During rehearsals and actual recording, standardized electronic media communication hand cues and signals should be used.

128

HAND CUES

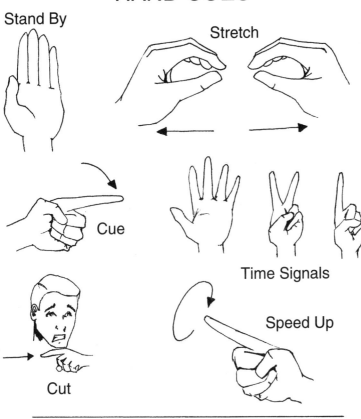

Stand By

Stretch

Cue

Time Signals

Speed Up

Cut

DIRECTOR'S VERBAL CUES

STAND BY   This is a call for quiet on the set or location, especially from the cast and crew. It means they must give the director their undivided attention and wait for the next cue.

ROLL TAPE   This is the cue to the tape or camera operator to start tape rolling and recording and must be followed by--

SPEED   (By the tape or camera operator)
This cue indicates to the director that the tape is rolling and recording, up to speed and locked in, ready for the call for action.

ACTION   This indicates to both the cast and crew to start their rehearsed action, speech, movement, etc.

CUT   This cue means to stop recording, acting, or any other action. It is an indication from the director that either the required material has been recorded or that something has gone wrong and to continue would be a waste of time.

Directing Talent

Once all of the physical setup procedures have begun, the director then concentrates on the human values that make up a production. Actual direction of actors is the most complex part of a director's job. The performance of an actor depends on many variables beyond the director's control. An actor's training, background, experience (both in acting and in life), and mental state during the shoot all affect a performance. First, the director must get to know as many of the aforementioned factors as possible in the short time usually available on an EFP shoot. The director must then blend this knowledge with the results of an in-depth study of the script and the plan he or she has for how to accomplish his or her interpretation of that script.

Interpersonal communication is the key to working with actors, who are in a very vulnerable position. It is their faces and voices that will be viewed by the audience. If the production comes off poorly, it is the actors that the audience will remember. The director must clearly communicate to the actor exactly what is needed, how it fits into the overall production, and how the actor will look and sound. For most actors, the more precise the direction provided, the better their performance. Without being condescending, a parent–child relationship often is the most workable type of relationship between a director and an actor.

Getting an emotional performance is the most difficult task for both the director and the actor. Once again, the actor must trust the director's judgment on how far to go in showing the type of emotion needed for a particular shot or scene. Often, actors are not aware that their reaction to other performers is as important as their own actions. This is the type of information a good director will impart to an actor as needed. Without delving into various acting approaches and methods, in general, actors perform better if they are aware of why they are doing what they have been asked to do. Supplying this motivation makes their job much easier and their acting much more realistic.

ACTOR–DIRECTOR RELATIONSHIP

Actress   Director

131

Shooting and Framing

A relationship of trust and communication must also exist between the director and camera operator. The director must trust the camera operator to frame, focus, and expose the shot as the director wants. Detailed communication between the director and the camera operator provides the best first step toward accomplishing a good relationship. If the camera operator understands what the director wants and needs in a shot, he or she is better equipped to provide the desired result.

Standard Shot Names

Starting with motion pictures and continuing over the years, the different placements of objects in the field of the camera, called *framing,* have acquired specific names. As in every aspect of media production, there are some variations in these names. The definitions discussed in this section are accepted and understood by all media professionals.

When the angle of view varies from the narrowest angle (tightest shot), it is called an *extreme close-up* (ECU) or *extra close-up* (XCU). A wider angle is a *close-up* (CU); the next widest angle is a *medium close-up* (MCU), followed by a *medium shot* (MS), *wide shot* (WS), and *extreme wide shot* (EWS) or *extra-wide shot* (XWS), the widest shot. Some directors call shots by specific framing; for example, a head-to-toe shot often is an MCU. Others prefer to make their shot variations in reference to the widest and/or narrowest shot. For example, in a football game, a shot of the entire field from a blimp is obviously an XWS, whereas a shot of the quarterback from the waist up is an XCU. However, in a television commercial where a football player holds a product in his hand, the XWS is a head-to-toe shot, and the XCU is the shot of the label of the product.

Other shots are named for the objects included in the field of view. A *two-shot* contains two objects, usually two people; a *three-shot* contains three objects. An *over-the-shoulder* (OS) shot is a shot in which part of the interviewer's shoulder appears in the foreground and the person being interviewed faces the camera. A *point-of-view* (POV) shot shows what a person in the scene sees from his or her position in the set.

An entire set of shots is named for their relative framing on the human body: *head shot, bust shot,* or *waist shot.* One caution on this type of nomenclature: No shot should cut objects off at logical cutoff points. If a human head is framed so that the bottom of the frame cuts off the head at the neck, it appears in the shot that the person has been decapitated. It is better to include just a small portion of the shoulders to indicate that the body continues.

SHOT FRAMING

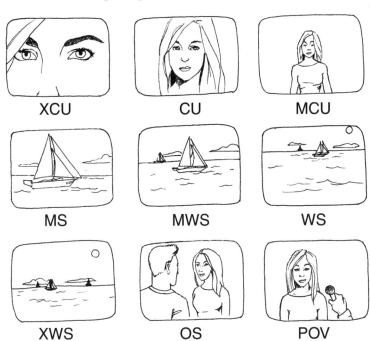

XCU   CU   MCU

MS   MWS   WS

XWS   OS   POV

CLOSURE THEORY

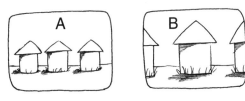

Frame "A" indicates three houses are present.
Frame "B" indicates more than three houses.

Framing Principles I

Aspect Ratio

The original video standard frame ratio has been 4 units wide by 3 units high (4 : 3 ratio). This means that to fill the video frame without exceeding its boundaries, the subject must fit into a horizontal rectangle 75% greater in width than height. This is an absolute. Turning the camera on its side to frame a predominately tall, slender subject results in an image that is laying on its side.

On the surface, this does not seem to offer much of a problem to a director or camera operator, but in reality, there are few objects that fit neatly into 4 : 3 space. Either some of the object must be cut off, or additional items must be added to the picture to create an acceptable composition. The 4 : 3 ratio becomes especially critical when shooting people. Unless a person is lying down, the human body does not fit into a 4 : 3 horizontal rectangle, nor do automobiles, most tall buildings, ships, airplanes, or any number of other everyday objects.

The new digital standard frame ratio currently in place for video is 16 : 9; that is, 16 units wide by 9 units high. This ratio is a compromise among several motion picture wide-screen frame ratios. Translation circuits are included in some cameras to enable equipment to be switched between ratios. As always with a major change in technology within an existing system, there will be a period for transition during which both ratios will be used. Digital equipment makes this transition much easier, because the ratio can be changed with a minor change in a digital circuit that controls the sweeps picking up the voltages from the camera chips. For the time being, most productions will be split between 4 : 3 ratio and some higher-quality network productions produced in 16 : 9 ratio. Digital Cinema is shot in 16 : 9, as are many commercials and music videos. All productions should be planned with both ratios in mind, because it will be several years before all receivers and consumer recording media will be able to view in both formats; therefore, all shooting should allow for conversion when necessary or required.

ASPECT RATIO – ESSENTIAL AREA

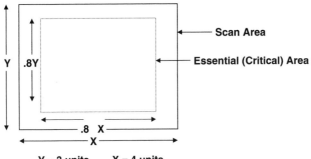

Y = 3 units   X = 4 units
Standard 4:3 NTSC Ratio

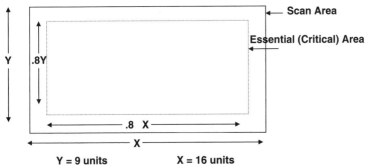

Y = 9 units   X = 16 units
Standard HDTV 16:9 ATSC Ratio

Framing Principles I

135

Framing Principles II

Critical Area

Besides the 4 : 3 or 16 : 9 horizontal aspect ratio, an additional framing problem exists in video. The entire video signal created by the camera does not reach the television receiver or monitor. In addition, the scanning sweeps of most receivers have increased because of age or misalignment. This means that as much as 5% to 10% of the picture cannot be seen by the audience. The 80% of the center portion of the frame is considered the critical or essential area (also called the safe title area). This 80% (allowing a 10% border on all four sides) is accepted by the industry as the critical area standard. All important information—names, addresses, phone numbers, and prices—should always be framed well within the critical area to ensure that all viewers receive it.

Any objects framed in the 10% border may be seen by some viewers, so unwanted objects should not be framed in this area, which is the *edge bleed area.* For sports or other action-oriented coverage, the acceptable framing limitations are slightly broader than the critical area, allowing approximately a 5% border. The center area for sports is called the safe action area. The difference in philosophy is that in an action sequence, closure fills in any portions of objects that momentarily appear beyond the critical area.

Lead Room or Edge Attraction

Psychological studies indicate that objects in the area near the edge of the frame create a different perception than those in the center of the frame. A major factor is called *edge attraction theory,* in which an object appears to move toward the edge, even if it remains stationary in the frame. This effect is increased when the object near the edge is a person's face. This lack of *nose room* makes the audience uncomfortable and should be avoided. The attraction of the edge is compounded when the subject is moving toward the edge. This is why moving objects should be given plenty of space ahead of them as the camera follows on a pan or tilt.

The Rule of Thirds

Related to the edge attraction theory is the artist's *rule of thirds,* which states that the most aesthetic location for a predominately vertical form is one third of the way in from either the left or right side of the frame. Conversely, the most aesthetic position for a predominately horizontal form is either one third of the way up from the bottom or down from the top of the frame. A quick review of classic artwork shows these framing rules being used extensively.

SUBJECT FRAMING RULES

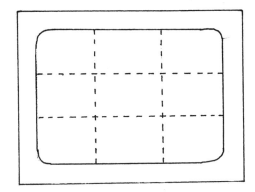

Rule of Thirds

Nose Room

Lead Room

Creating Movement I

Even though video is a moving art form, the individual frame is essentially a still photograph. The manner in which each picture is framed can add to or subtract from its perceived movement. There are three basic means of creating movement in either video or film: by moving the subject, by moving the camera, and by editing. Within each of these three basic movements are ancillary movements.

Subject Movement

Subjects can move in three directions within the frame: on the horizontal (X-axis) or vertical (Y-axis) planes in front of the camera or moving toward or away (Z-axis) from the camera. Z-axis movements are the most powerful and should be used judiciously. Moving from left to right (X-axis) in our culture suggests moving ahead; conversely, moving to the left signifies returning or backing up. The Y-axis movements are more complex and less universally accepted, except that movement from the upper left to the lower right implies the most powerful movement forward, except for straight toward the camera.

Interestingly, the cultural values attributed to these movements also affect the relative value of positions within the frame. If the frame is divided into nine areas—upper left, upper center, upper right, middle left, center, middle right, lower left, lower center, and lower right—the position considered the most beneficial for passing information to the audience is the lower right. This conclusion is based on the philosophy that, in our culture, the eye starts at the upper left, proceeds to the lower right, and comes to rest there. For that reason, ego-centered television program hosts usually insist on being framed on the right; higher-quality newscasts place the visuals on the right; and, almost universally, prices, addresses, and other critical commercial information are framed on the right.

FRAME AXIS

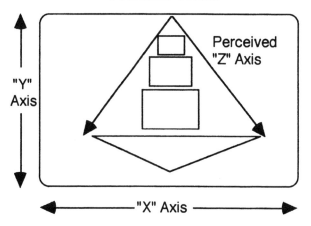

"Y" Axis

Perceived "Z" Axis

—— "X" Axis ——

DOMINANT MOVEMENT

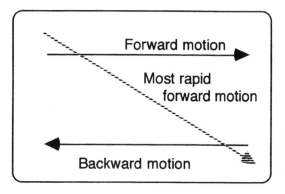

Forward motion

Most rapid forward motion

Backward motion

Final eye resting area

139

Creating Movement II

Camera Movement

The second way to create movement is by moving the camera: on its pan head, panning left or right, or tilting up or down. If the camera has a means of raising or lowering on a center shaft, this movement is called *pedestaling* up or down. Whether the camera base is a tripod on dolly wheels, a pedestal mount with wheels, a wheeled dolly, crab, or crane mount, the movements may be a *dolly* in or out, a *truck* left or right, or a combination of both to move in an arc. The crane mount also permits additional combinations of movement up, down, in, out, left, and right.

Movement through Zooms

Supplementary movement created within the lens is the zoom. A zoom movement is created by varying the focal length of the lens, which increases or decreases the angle of view. The zoom, especially with a motorized control, is an easy and flexible movement. However, it is an unrealistic movement and should be used with great caution. Amateur videographers use the zoom instead of planning in advance and using other aspects of professional video production open to those who have studied and learned to use them.

In addition, digital cameras can "digitally" zoom by enlarging the pixels. At a certain point in the zoom, the quality of the picture degenerates.

The zoom does not change the perspective of a shot, meaning that as the angle narrows and the picture appears to become larger, the camera's angle is not closer. Instead, it shows a smaller portion of the picture. A dolly can achieve the same movement and is more realistic, because as the camera moves closer to the subject, the perspective also changes. Although even the most professional film and video camera operators now use zoom lenses, they do not use them during a shot. Instead, they use the zoom lens as it was intended to be used, as a way to vary the focal length of the lens without changing lenses.

Zooms during a shot may be used on a flat, two-dimensional object, because there is no perspective involved, or as a special effect. But like all special effects, a zoom should be used sparingly and with specifically planned intent other than just tightening or loosening a shot.

CAMERA MOVEMENTS

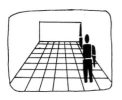 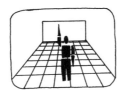 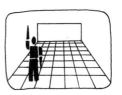

Panning to the Right

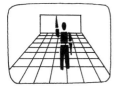 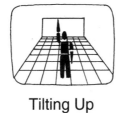 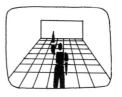

Dollying to the Right

 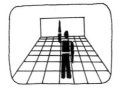 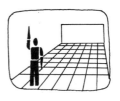

Tilting Up

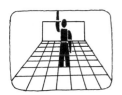  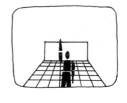

Pedestaling Up

141

Creating Z-Axis Movement

Video, like painting, photography, and cinematography, is a two-dimensional art form. The picture has only a height and width as received on a receiver/monitor or shown on a screen. The depth, or third dimension, of the picture is perceived; it does not actually exist as a third dimension, but it appears to exist. This three-dimensional appearance is important to any visual medium. Video particularly depends on the Z-axis to compensate for its smaller screen and lower resolution compared with photography or motion picture film.

Therefore, it is imperative that the camera operator and director specifically think about and design the shots so that the Z-axis is exploited to its maximum. Applying all the creative techniques disclosed in the preceding sections furnishes the means to do so.

Moving subjects in the frame or moving the camera around the subjects; arranging the objects in patterns that appear to be in perspective; using as short a focal length lens as possible; and arranging objects and subjects in the frame to create a background, middle ground, and foreground all help create a usable Z-axis. Lining up objects in front of the camera in neat rows, equal distance from the camera, and placing all objects on surfaces of the same height, size, and/or color decrease the appearance of the Z-axis.

Arranging objects in the frame so that, even at rest, there appears to be movement, by using the object's graphic forces, also improves the three-dimensional perception. Do not shoot a person or object straight on. This is not only boring, but it adds weight and width to that person. Instead, rotate the person so that the camera is getting a three-quarter view, but do not turn the person so far that both eyes are no longer visible. Avoid having two people stand next to each other while talking to the camera or each other; place them so that they are facing each other, with the camera shooting past first one and then the other.

Z-AXIS DO'S & DON'TS

Don't

Do

Don't

Do

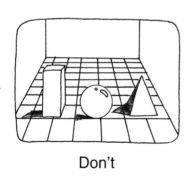

Don't

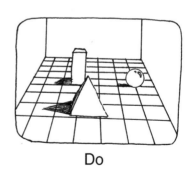

Do

Graphic Forces

Another aesthetic theory to be considered when framing a shot is the *graphic weight* of the objects within the frame. Each discernible object has some graphic weight or value. A large, dark object has a greater weight than a small, light-colored object. An object with jagged, irregular edges has more weight than an object with smooth, rounded edges. Two small objects may equal the weight of one large one, even though their actual square measurement might be slightly smaller.

In addition to the perceived graphic weight of an object is its graphic force. The *graphic force* is derived partially from its graphic weight and also from its movement. An object at rest has less graphic force than an object moving across the frame. An object or series of objects that appear to be moving also have increased graphic weight. Objects shaped like an arrow, a row of objects arranged to lead the eye in a specific direction, or a series of shots that show an object in a position of potential movement carry more graphic force than an object of the same size without the same graphic forces present.

Color also becomes a factor in determining the weight of an object. Objects colored in "hot" colors such as red, yellow, orange, and light versions of other colors tend to extend toward the viewer. These colors appear to be lighter in graphic weight. The "cool" colors such as blue, violet, and green and darker versions of other colors tend to recede from the viewer. These colors appear to be heavier in graphic weight.

In the midst of all these "rules," remember that there are no absolutes in any aesthetic field. All of the suggestions made in this section are intended to be used only as guidelines. Each individual production situation determines to what extent these suggestions are followed or ignored. The resulting final production will chronicle whether the best choices were made.

GRAPHIC FORCES

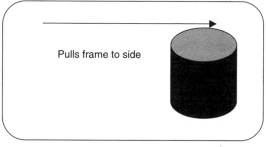

Pulls frame to side

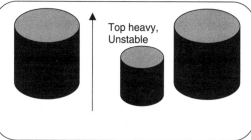

Top heavy, Unstable

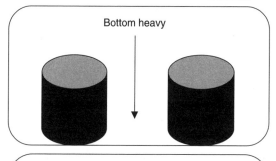

Bottom heavy

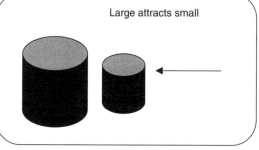

Large attracts small

Shooting to Edit: The Third Movement

Regardless of the skill of the camera operator and director in planning and framing shots, unless the shots have been recorded to be edited together, all the aesthetic values will be lost. In EFP production, each shot is recorded separately and often out of order. To later assemble the shots in a meaningful manner close to the original intent of the production, they must be shot with editing in mind.

First, consider the *electronic aspect*. Because linear editors require some preroll space before making an edit, there must be at least 5 seconds of uninterrupted sync pulses and control track (if it is a CT editor) pulses preceding the edit entry point; that is, after the director has called for the tape to roll, a full 5 seconds must elapse before any usable action is recorded. At the end of the take, another 5 seconds should be recorded as protection after the director has called "Cut." For nonlinear editing, preroll is not as critical, but head and tail footage is always appreciated by any editor, regardless of the editing method.

Second, consider the *practical aspect*. Each shot should be recorded so that its action overlaps both the preceding and the following shot. This allows the editor greater protection in the event that a shot did not start or end exactly as intended. This overlap also gives the director a wider range of choices as to the best segment of an action to cut.

The third aspect to consider is the *continuity aspect*. To edit in a seamless fashion, continuity must be maintained. The action from one shot must flow into the action of the next shot, unless there is a transition or change of scene. To avoid discontinuity problems, shots are recorded overlapping each other to offer the editor a choice in where to make the edit. There are three basic types of continuity that generally must be matched in each edit: continuity of action, direction, and location.

EDITING PATTERNS

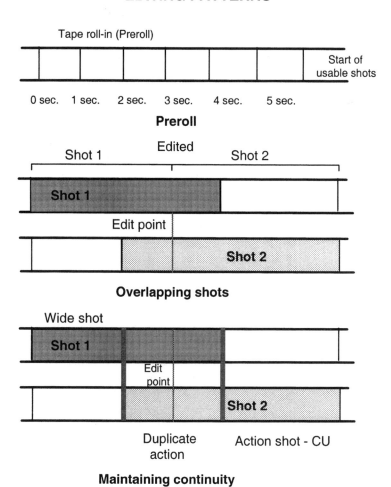

Tape roll-in (Preroll)

Start of
usable shots

0 sec. 1 sec. 2 sec. 3 sec. 4 sec. 5 sec.

Preroll

Shot 1

Edited

Shot 2

Shot 1

Edit point

Shot 2

Overlapping shots

Wide shot

Shot 1

Edit
point

Shot 2

Duplicate
action

Action shot - CU

Maintaining continuity

147

The Three Types of Continuity

Continuity of Action

As the actor picks up the pencil in the WS, the CU must be shot so that the rate of picking up the pencil is the same and the same hand and pencil are used. This seems like a logical action, but even the best directors and camera operators make action continuity mistakes. For that reason, a *continuity assistant* (CA), also known as a *script supervisor,* is an essential member of any major production crew. The CA watches every shot carefully and records the action on a script, or even takes digital still or instant photos of the beginning and ending of each shot to check continuity. Because most major productions are videotaped while being shot on film, a quick replay of the tape can answer most continuity questions.

Continuity of Direction

If the WS shows the actor facing to the left and the actor's right hand reaches across the frame to the left, then the CU must show the hand moving to the left. If a shot shows an actor moving to the right, then the next shot must show the same actor still moving to the right, unless there is a change of direction shown on camera in the shot or a cutaway is inserted between the two shots. A cutaway can confuse the audience, however, if they remember that the actor was moving in one direction, but is then seen moving in the opposite direction in the next shot in which he or she appears. A straight-on shot from directly in front of or from the rear of the actor also can be used as a transition. This same rule applies to all movement, whether it involves automobiles; airplanes; people walking, running, or falling; or objects being thrown or dropped or moving on their own. Psychologically, movement from the left to right is a forward movement, whereas movement from right to left is a returning movement.

Continuity of Location

Continuity of location includes lighting, background, and audio. If the establishing shot is lit in low key with heavy shadows, then all of the CUs must be lit the same way. If one shot shows the ocean in the background, then, unless there is a change of direction shown on camera, all shots should indicate the ocean is the background. Audio continuity becomes an aesthetic tool, as well as a continuity rule. If the scene is in a large, empty hall, all the audio must sound as if it were recorded in the same ambiance. However, the ambiance of a WS in the same location sounds different from that of a tight CU of two people talking and standing close to each other.

148

SHOOTING FOR EDITING

shot 1   shot 2

Continuity of Action
(cut-in)

shot 1   shot 2

Continuity of Direction

shot 1   shot 2

Continuity of Location

Cover Shots

There are three types of cover shots that are the friends and saviors of the editor: *cover, cutaway,* and *cut-in shots.* Any capable director will call for them to be recorded, and any professional camera operator will shoot them even if the director forgets to do so.

A cover shot is an illustration of what is being talked about or referred to. If an announcer speaks of the use of a product, then a shot of the product being used in that manner is a cover shot. The announcer does not need to and probably should not appear in the shot. Instead of a single shot, a series of shots or a sequence would better illustrate what the announcer is talking about.

Cutaway and cut-in shots are similar, except that a cutaway is a shot of items that are not included in the previous or following shots; for example, two people are sitting and talking in a railway station, and then a shot of the train arriving is shown. The characters do not refer to it (if they did, it would be a cover shot), and most important, they must be sitting in a position where they are not included in the shot of the train. But the audience realizes this train has something to do with the action. Generally, cutaway shots provide two important characteristics of a sequence. First, the shot gives the audience information that the main action does not reveal. Second, it can be used to cover an edit that would be a jump cut unless an intervening shot can be inserted.

A cut-in is a CU of some object that is visible in the preceding or following frame. If a woman's purse is visible in a CU as two characters sit in the train station, then it is a cut-in shot if the purse is also visible in the WS.

These three types of shots afford the editor the chance to correct mistakes made in the shooting continuity; they can also be used as a way to speed up or slow down a sequence or to correct a continuity problem in the production.

COVER SHOTS

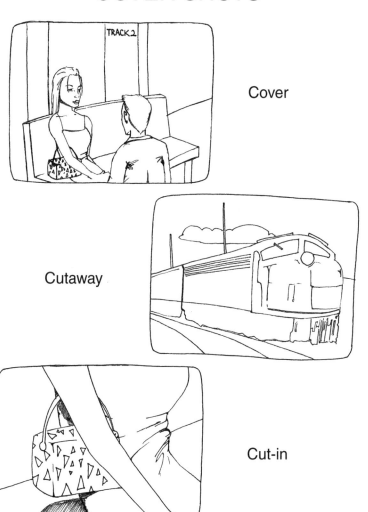

Cover

Cutaway

Cut-in

151

In-Camera Effects I

Technology exists that allows you to produce a series of special effects simply by using the controls necessary for the normal operation of a camera. Depending on the quality and level of the recorder, some effects may be produced by its operation. As technology advances, newer cameras have digital special effects capabilities built into them.

Any professional analog camera and many consumer camcorders are capable of producing special effects such as iris fades, rack focus, swish pans/zooms, reverse polarity, and manipulation of pedestal and gain (including electronic pedestal).

Iris Fades

An *iris fade-in* or *fade-out* is created by placing the iris control on manual and setting the iris opening stopped all the way down. With the recorder rolling, the iris may be slowly opened up and brought to the proper setting, thus creating a fade-in. A fade-out is created by reversing the procedure: A scene is started with the recorder rolling and the iris set properly. At the right moment, the iris is stopped down until the picture fades to black. Neither of these effects works well unless the light level is low enough that the iris is almost completely wide open at the proper setting.

Rack Focus

To *rack focus* simply means to start a scene in focus and rapidly turn the focus control until the picture is totally out of focus. The shot to be edited next should start totally out of focus and, on cue, roll into proper focus. Again, this effect works well only when the light level is low enough that the depth of field is quite shallow, and the focus change should be rapid enough to appear intentional, not an error in shooting.

Swish Pans and Zooms

A *swish pan* is accomplished by starting on a scene, and then at the end of the shot, quickly panning the camera at a high enough rate to blur the image. The next shot starts with a fast pan and ends properly framed. The first of these tasks is easy to accomplish, but for the second, it is difficult to stop at the exact framing without jerking or missing the mark.

A *swish zoom* is a little easier to execute, especially if the zoom is motorized. The process is the same as a swish pan in that the shot starts at a normal focal length, but then, on cue, the zoom control is operated at its maximum speed, usually zooming in rather than out. The second shot starts with a zoom out and ends properly framed.

IN-CAMERA EFFECTS

Swish Pan

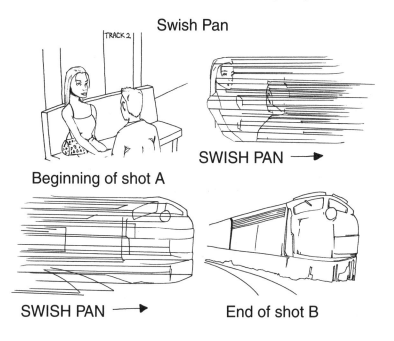

Beginning of shot A

SWISH PAN ➝

SWISH PAN ➝

End of shot B

153

In-Camera Effects II

Digital In-Camera Effects

If the camera has built-in digital circuits, it may be possible to solarize, freeze, or pixilate the picture, among many other effects, depending on the individual camera. The *solarization* effect causes the image to appear as if it is melting or reversing in polarity. A freeze effect locks a single frame of the picture as if it were a still photo. *Pixilation* is the process of removing a certain number of frames of the picture so that objects and subjects appear to move about in an irregular, jerky fashion. Each of these effects requires a separate control on the camera to produce the indicated effect. Pixilation can also be accomplished if the tape deck can record a single frame at a time. A control, usually labeled *intervalometer,* sets the number of frames per second at which the recorder will operate. This compresses the action in any time elapsed required for the production.

Pedestal and Variable Gain Manipulation

Two other electronic controls, usually located internally on the camera, are the *pedestal* and *variable gain controls*. All cameras have a gain control easily located on the outside of the camera, but it is a step switch that gives the operator a choice of setting several different gain levels in the video amplifier. This switch allows the operator to compensate for low light levels by boosting the gain internally. Although the gain boost makes the picture brighter, it also increases the noise level in the picture.

The *internal gain control* is a potentiometer that allows continuous gain settings. The *pedestal control* changes the black level or contrast of the picture.

Use caution when manipulating either the pedestal or internal gain controls. Once either of these controls has been changed, it probably requires a test signal, oscilloscope, and a technician to return the camera to its normal operating condition. Therefore, changing these controls should be done only for extreme production needs.

Reversing Polarity

Reversing polarity is achieved by throwing a switch, internally or externally depending on the camera. This cannot be done while you are recording because there is a momentary loss of synchronization. The picture areas that were red become cyan, areas that were green become magenta, blue areas become yellow, and vice versa. Light areas become dark and dark areas become light. The effect is the same as looking at a color film negative.

All in-camera effects can be accomplished more effectively through the camera's camera control unit or, in some cases, during postproduction.

154

CAMERA CONTROL EFFECTS

Reverse Polarity

Normal Picture

Picture with Reverse Polarity

Continuity Records: Logging

A manual operation often overlooked in the focus on electronic operations in a video production is the continuity record keeping or logging process. A written record of each shot is kept on a log sheet in a form that supplies the director and the editor with the information they need to accomplish their tasks. The log registers, in the order of shooting, the shot and take number and the location on the medium (that is, counter, SMPTE time code, or elapsed time). Comments on whether the audio, video, or both were good and why and any other comments the director wants noted also are listed.

The log is invaluable to the editor. If not accurately logged during the shoot, the cassettes, discs, or drives must be previewed and logged in real time during postproduction—a slow and painstaking procedure. One person, whose main responsibility is logging, should keep the logs; this person's title in a large crew may be "continuity assistant" or "secretary." In a smaller crew, the director or an assigned production assistant may be in charge of logging. The importance of this function cannot be ignored. The person keeping the log must be familiar with the critical aspects of continuity and well versed in that particular production.

The CA has a copy of the shot sheet, which indicates the order the shots will be set up and recorded, and a copy of the latest revision of the script. It is helpful to the log keeper to attend the preshoot production meetings to become intimately aware of all aspects of the production.

As each shot is set up and rehearsed, the logger notes positions of props, set pieces, lighting, or anything else that may be moved or changed. Because the production will be shot out of sequence, hours or days may separate the actual shooting of some shots in the same sequence, and every aspect of each shot must match to maintain continuity. As each shot is completed, the CA logs any deviations from the script and minute details, such as which hand an actor used to handle a prop. A digital still camera is invaluable to a CA; after each shot, the director, camera operator, and audio operator dictate comments to be added to the log. Each cassette, disc, or drive has a separate log page, and often each unit may have more than one log page. The pages should be labeled accurately to match the labels on the cassettes, discs, and drives. If copies are available, one copy goes in the box with the medium, another is kept with the assistant's files, and a third is delivered to the director.

If the editing is done on a nonlinear digital editor, the logs become even more important. The tedious, time-consuming activity of real-time dubbing all the footage into a digital format before editing can be reduced by converting only those shots good enough for the final production. All other shots are left in original form to be dubbed later, if they are needed.

156

RECORDER LOG

RECORDER LOG PAGE _____   DATE _____

LOCATION _____ PRODUCTION _____

CAMERA/RECORDER _____ REEL # _____

PRODUCER _____ DIRECTOR _____ OPERATOR _____

TIME CODE	TAKE	DESCRIPTION	REMARKS

Continuity Records: Logging

157

Striking

After the excitement of the actual production has evaporated and the actors, directors, and producers have disappeared, the last stage of the production process beings. This stage is just as important as any other stage, but it occurs when everyone is tired and let down after the tension of the shoot has eased and everyone is thinking about tomorrow.

As soon as the order to *strike* (a term borrowed from the theater) has been given by the director, or the production manager on a larger crew, all power is killed, except for any work lights that are present. Then, all other cables are disconnected to prevent crew members from tripping over them and pulling equipment or lighting instruments down. Each crew person has striking equipment responsibility. Cables are properly coiled and stored in their cases. Once equipment has been cleaned and returned to the proper cases, a check is made to ensure that all equipment has been packed and is ready to be loaded.

The strike should be as organized as the setup. The next use of the equipment may come the following day. Note any damaged equipment in writing and notify maintenance immediately. The location has to be restored to its original condition. You should repair any damage or report it to the owners in writing and negotiate a satisfactory compensation before you leave the site.

Equipment is then moved to the vehicle, loaded, and returned to its storage locations. Each piece of equipment must be carefully checked with the person responsible, whether it is the production manager or a leasing company. Take the same precautionary measures during striking as you did during the setup. Never leave equipment or the equipment vehicle unattended until all equipment has been secured.

The "fun" part of the production has now ended. It consumed the shortest period, and, in many ways, the least amount of effort, at least mental and aesthetic effort. Once you have worked several EFPs, you will appreciate the physical effort required for the production process.

STRIKE LIST

1. CAP CAMERA

2. TURN OFF ALL POWER SWITCHES EXCEPT WORK LIGHTS

3. DISMISS TALENT

4. DISCONNECT ALL CABLES, BOTH ENDS

5. LOWER ALL LIGHT STANDS, MOVE GENTLY OUT OF THE
   WAY TO COOL

6. PICK UP AND PACK ALL PROPS, SET PIECES
   LOAD SETS, LARGE SET PIECES

7. COIL CABLES PROPERLY, OVER-UNDER,
   NOT AROUND ELBOW

8. WIPE DOWN CABLES AND SECURELY FASTEN ENDS

9. REMOVE CAMERA FROM TRIPOD,
   PACK IN CASE WITH ACCESSORIES
   (TRIPOD PLATE, POWER PACK) THAT BELONG IN CASE

10. PACK ALL CABLES, BATTERIES

11. PACK ALL GAFFER EQUIPMENT

12. IF COOL, DISMANTLE LAMP HEADS AND STANDS
    THEN PACK

13. INVENTORY ALL EQUIPMENT CASES
    AND LOOSE EQUIPMENT

14. MOVE EQUIPMENT TO VEHICLE
    ** NEVER LEAVE ANY EQUIPMENT UNATTENDED **

15. LOAD EQUIPMENT INTO VEHICLE

Striking

159

The Production Process: Postproduction

The Editing Function

As the final stage of the video production process, postproduction affords the last opportunity to reach the goal originally set by the client. Regardless of the saying, "Fix it in post," not all errors in judgment, miscalculations, and poor production techniques can be corrected in postproduction. If the material is not available or is technically deficient, there may be no way to replace it or to rectify the problems created in preproduction and/or production.

Most editors believe the truly creative portion of video production takes place in the editing room, and many directors and producers agree. Video editing is a function that requires a combination of technical and aesthetic knowledge and unlimited patience.

The technical factors depend on the capabilities of the equipment available for the editing session. A good editor knows the limits of the equipment and can use those limits without creating technical problems. The aesthetic factors call on knowledge of psychology, art, music, theater, and all performing arts. Editing is often a long, tedious process that stretches even the most patient people to their limit.

Linear Editing Systems

The equipment used to edit videotape ranges from two videotape decks connected for dubbing to the most complex, computer-controlled, all-digital, nonlinear systems. Linear editors use *control track* (CT) and/or *time code* (TC) editing as a means of controlling the tape decks and determining the location of the edits.

In linear editing suites, there are at least three pieces of equipment: a controller, a source deck, and a record deck. More complex suites may use more than one source deck with *time base correctors* (TBCs), a video switcher, character and graphic generators, and an audio control board with a complement of audio sources.

Audio Sources

An audio control board is not an absolute requirement for a simple linear editing suite, but some means of setting audio levels should be included in the system. A more satisfactory system includes an audio board that feeds the outputs of both the audio tracks from each of the source decks plus audio tape decks, turntable, compact disc (CD) player, and microphone outputs through the board. This setup allows you to mix more than one audio source and controls the levels and the equalization of the audio, if the board has this design feature.

162

CUTS-ONLY LINEAR EDITING

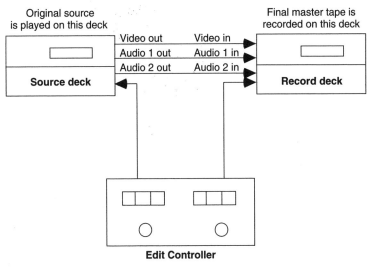

Original source
is played on this deck

Final master tape is
recorded on this deck

Video out   Video in
Audio 1 out   Audio 1 in
Audio 2 out   Audio 2 in

Source deck

Record deck

Edit Controller

Controls shuttle, preroll,
and playback functions
of source deck

Controls shuttle, prerecord,
play, and record functions
of record deck

The Editing Function

163

Editing System Components

Controller

The controller is a specialized computer designed to perform three functions: controlling the playback functions of the source deck, controlling the play and record functions of the record deck, and storing this information. Controllers have a time readout that indicates the position of each tape in each deck. This time indicator on a CT system merely counts the CT pulses as they pass by a pickup head. In a TC system, the indicator reads the exact position of the tape, because the TC address is recorded directly onto the tape.

A controller uses either a knob or joystick as a method of shuttling the tapes back and forth. A single control can be assigned to an individual machine as needed, or there may be shuttle controls for each machine in the system. The standard Play, Record, Fast Forward, Rewind, and Stop buttons for each machine also appear on the controller. In addition, controls specifically designed for editing functions include a method of choosing between assemble or insert editing; switches to choose recording of either or both audio tracks and/or the video track in the insert editing mode; a method of indicating the entry and exit edit points on the source machine(s) and recorder; and, depending on the editor, switches that allow for previewing an edit without recording it, double-checking the entry and exit points, and reviewing the edit after it has been recorded.

Video Sources

The *source deck* (also called the *player*) and the *recorder deck* (sometimes known as the *editor*) are special videotape decks with additional circuits that allow the machines to be locked together in synchronization (sync). The controls on the decks are the same as on any tape deck, but there are ports for connecting cables to the controller that are not present on a standard tape deck. If the controller can handle more than one source deck, then a TBC for each source deck must be used to lock the recorders in sync so that a switcher can be used to record transitions other than cuts. Without TBCs and a switcher, cuts are the only transition possible.

If character and/or graphic generators and a camera are included as additional sources, they may be used through a switcher as long as they are gen-locked to the system. *Gen-locking* is the process of tying all of the synchronous signals of the tape decks to the same time reference so that shots can be freely combined through a switcher without causing the picture to lose sync and roll uncontrollably.

164

A-B ROLL LINEAR EDITING

Source deck 1

Audio inputs:
mics, tape,
CD, etc

Source deck 2

Video
out to
switcher

Audio out
to mixer

Audio out
to mixer

Video
out to
switcher

Audio mixer

Audio 1 | Audio 2

Audio inputs to
record deck

Record deck

Video input to
record deck

Video switcher

Control signal
to source deck 1
from edit
controller

Control signal
to source deck 2
from edit
controller

A-B roll edit controller

Linear Editing Methods: Technical

Two types of technical edits can be made using linear editing equipment: an assemble edit and an insert edit.

Assemble Edit

An assemble edit records the video track, both audio tracks, and the CT simultaneously. This offers a quick and simple method of editing one shot after another, but it prevents you from editing the video separately from either of the audio tracks or any combination of the three.

Insert Edit

An insert edit allows you to freely edit any of the three tracks separately, together, or in any combination. To achieve an insert edit, a continuous series of the CT pulses must be recorded first. This process is called *laying down CT, black burst,* or *color bars.* To lay down a continuous series of CTs, a complete video signal (no audio signal is needed) must be recorded on the tape.

One method, black burst, involves recording a black level signal from a signal generator or a switcher, or the signal from a capped camera. Another method is to record a color bar signal from a generator, switcher, or camera generating a color bar output. The signal must be continuous if the editing is to be accomplished on a CT editor. If the editing is being done on a TC editor, a TC signal is recorded in the vertical interval portion of the video signal (VITC), on a special TC track, or on an unused audio track at the same time as the black burst or color bars.

The choice of whether to record black or color bars on the video track depends on the final use of the tape. For master tapes that probably will not be duplicated, such as news stories, black is usually laid down. If a slight error is made in an edit that leaves a one- or two-frame gap between edits, the black will not be readily visible when the original master is played. However, if several generations of dubs are to be made with a frame or two of black, it may show as a flash or picture roll. When color bars are used, any gap between shots is easily seen at the time the tape is edited or previewed before dubs are made. Most professional postproduction facilities use color bars when laying down TC or CT.

Once black or color bar signals have been laid down, a professional editor seldom finds any need to edit using anything other than the insert mode. If CT or sync pulses are accidentally erased or damaged, an assemble edit will be necessary to restore the continuity of both pulses, but the edit will have to continue beyond the length of the finished production or additional assemble edits will need to be made.

166

EDIT TRACK ARRANGEMENTS

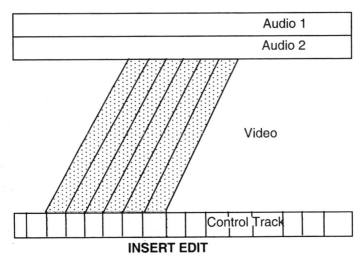

| | Audio 1 |
| | Audio 2 |

Video

Control Track

ASSEMBLE EDIT

Simultaneous recording of audio, video, and
control track. CANNOT record tracks separately.
Does not sync with prerecorded material at end of edit.

| Audio 1 |
| Audio 2 |

Video

Control Track

INSERT EDIT

May record audio 1, audio 2, or video tracks individually
or any combination of those three tracks.
DOES NOT re-record prerecorded control track.
Makes seamless edits and exits regardless of track choices.

Linear Editing Operating Methods

Every studio, facility, and station has a standard operating procedure (SOP) that designates the exact format to be used in laying down black burst, color bars, tone, and slate and for labeling of reels, cassettes, and boxes. This section is a compilation of an SOP that demonstrates the purposes of each segment of the operation.

Shuttle a new tape in fast-forward beyond the length of the antici-pated edited master. Then rewind the tape to the beginning and reset the timer or TC reader to determine the beginning of the tape. Except for recording bars or black burst, no usable programming material should be recorded at the very beginning of a reel or cassette. Next, run the tape for 30 to 60 seconds to ensure that the tape stock is beyond any dirt that might have been picked up or any damaged tape that sometimes exists at the start of a tape cassette or reel.

Lay down 30 to 60 seconds of 1,000 Hz tone with bars as video. If these two test signals are not set at the exact levels to be used in the recording, they will be useless. These test signals are used by the tech-nician preparing to play the tape back to set the playback levels and adjust for tracking, skew, and other electronic adjustments. Following the tone and bars, record about 10 seconds of a slate that specifies the title, length, client, date of recording, and, if a dub, which generation. Next, record a countdown with descending numbers from 10 to 2, followed by a minimum of 2 seconds of clean black and silence before the beginning of the first audio and video of the first shot of the edited production.

At the end of the production, record at least 10 seconds of clean black and silence. These periods of clean black and silence furnish a guard band of neutral signals in the event that there are errors in switch-ing during a playback; they also provide a logical space for dubbing.

EDIT DECISION LIST-MASTER TAPE SIGNALS

PRODUCTION _____   **PAGE** _____

PRODUCER _____ **EDITOR** _____ **DATE** _____

EDIT #	REEL	DESCRIPTION	VIDEO IN/OUT	AUDIO IN/OUT

MASTER TAPE SIGNALS

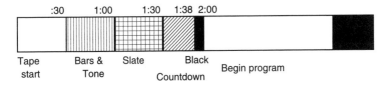

:30	1:00	1:30	1:38 2:00

Tape start   Bars & Tone   Slate   Black   Countdown   Begin program

Master tapes for duplication and video disc masters
require special signals for precise dubs. Check with
duplication facility for their specifications.

Linear Editing Operating Methods

Editing Steps

Regardless of the level or complexity of the equipment used, the editing process consists of four basic steps: previewing the raw footage, physically preparing the master reel or computer session, laying down shots, and recording and labeling the final production tape or computer disc.

If a nonlinear system is used, these same steps reduce the time required to load the original footage onto a computer's memory. The edit decision list (EDL) provides a means to choose only the critical and necessary shots required to be digitized for the project.

Assuming that you, as the editor, were not present during the shooting of the material and that accurate logs were kept, your first action is to review all of the raw footage. Then follow the logs and the script to begin to assimilate the material and reach an understanding of how the director interpreted the script with the shots recorded. If accurate logs were not kept during shooting, you must carefully preview the tape or computer files (called bins, derived from film terminology) and create a set of logs. If you were on the set at the time of shooting, the previewing process can be completed rapidly because you are already familiar with the footage that was shot. *— FIG 6.5 - EDL lop*

Efficient Editing

One method of decreasing the cost of editing and increasing the efficiency of the process is to create window dubs of the raw footage on a less expensive format with matching TC numbers. Video Home System (VHS) is popular for most projects; professional ½-inch format is desirable if the production was shot on a digital professional format. The window dub may be used to make a preliminary edited master away from an editing suite.

Once the EDL is complete, either handwritten or computerized, and the original raw footage is taken to a fully equipped editing suite, an edited master is created. If the EDL is computer generated, the list is entered into the online computer; the tapes are cued up on a series of playback machines; and the computer then proceeds to make all of the edits, including transitions, special effects, and split edits. If the EDL was made carefully, then the online master can be edited automatically in a short time, saving time and money.

EDIT DECISION LIST PROCESS

1. CHECK LABELS ON RAW FOOTAGE FROM SHOOT
   CREATE LABELS IF NONE ATTACHED

2. RECORD TIME CODE ON VITC, EXTRA AUDIO TRACK,
   OR SPECIAL TC TRACK IF NOT CODED WHEN RECORDED

3. DUB RAW FOOTAGE AND TIME CODE
   TO WINDOW DUB STOCK

4. PREVIEW AND LOG (OR CHECK LOGS) OF ALL FOOTAGE

5. EDIT OFF-LINE VERSION NOTING ALL EDIT POINTS
   (REEL NUMBER, EDIT NUMBER, ENTRY, EXIT POINTS,
   TRANSITION, AUDIO EDITS, AND SPECIAL EFFECTS)
   ON COMPUTER DISC, TAPE,
   OR MANUAL EDIT DECISION LIST

6. SEND ORIGINAL TAPE, OFF-LINE MASTER, AND EDL
   TO ON-LINE FACILITY

7. FOOTAGE WILL BE CUED ON MULTIPLE PLAYBACK
   DECKS AND COMPUTER WILL CONTROL ALL EDITING
   INSTRUCTIONS AS INDICATED ON THE EDL

8. NONLINEAR: DIGITIZE REQUIRED FOOTAGE USING
   EDIT DECISION LIST

9. ASSEMBLE SEQUENCES AND COMPLETE PROJECT

Editing Steps

Nonlinear Editing: Technical

This section discusses the difference between linear and nonlinear editing. Until recently, videotape could be edited only in a linear manner; that is, each shot was added to the preceding shot. Changes could be made in either audio or video in previously edited sequences only if the overall length was not shortened or lengthened. Unlike film, which is edited in a nonlinear manner, a shot could be cut out or added at any point simply by splicing in a new shot or by cutting out an unwanted shot and resplicing at the removed shot in the film. Video editing does not involve physically cutting and splicing; therefore, if a shot must be shortened or lengthened, all shots after the changed shot must be reedited.

Nonlinear editing involves the following six basic steps:

1. Logging footage
2. Digitizing footage
3. Capturing footage
4. Assembling footage
5. Rendering file(s)
6. Outputting files

Nonlinear editing also depends on three factors not included in linear editing:

1. All edits are virtual; that is, no footage is actually used in the edit, only in and out points recorded in the application's memory. Actual assembling of the clips (shots) does not occur until the rendering stage.
2. Because of the possible massive amount of memory required to digitize, manipulate, and render video clips, compression levels are critical to the quality of the final output and the amount of memory available or required. Compression is the process of digitizing only the critical portions of the video signal. Several compression systems are currently in use; the most common system for video is called MPEG. Since MPEG compression was first introduced, several different systems have evolved, each with a designator number such as MPEG-1 and MPEG-2. MPEG compression avoids digitizing any duplication between video frames, thereby saving memory space.
3. All material to be edited—audio, video, and graphics—must be in a common digital format to be edited nonlinearly. The material may be "captured" by any of three methods: by feeding directly from a digital camera through a FireWire or Serial Digital Interface (SDI) to the computer editing application, by feeding analog signals to a capture card installed in the computer, or by feeding the signal from a digital deck or passing an analog signal through a digital deck.

DIGITIZING FROM SHOOTING TO OUTPUT

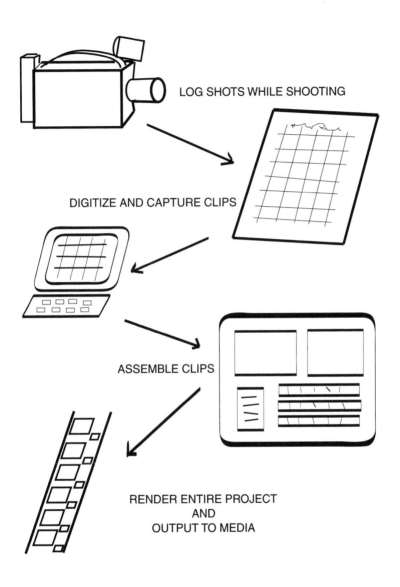

LOG SHOTS WHILE SHOOTING

DIGITIZE AND CAPTURE CLIPS

ASSEMBLE CLIPS

RENDER ENTIRE PROJECT
AND
OUTPUT TO MEDIA

Nonlinear Editing: Technical

173

Nonlinear Editing: Operating Methods

The nonlinear editing process starts in the same manner as all professional editing situations: with the shooting process. Keeping accurate logs at the time of recording the original footage makes the editing process simpler and more professional. If the footage is not accurately logged, then a logging session is necessary. All footage must be viewed on either the original footage or on a window dub. A *window dub* is a lower quality copy of the original footage with a window showing the TC as a reference in the lower third of the frame. This saves wear and tear on the original footage and may be accomplished on a consumer deck. Each shot needs to be logged with the in and out points and a brief description or title. This list becomes an EDL or batch list. If all of the footage is logged accurately with TC lists, then the digitizing process may proceed. As the footage is captured, it is stored in a bin in the computer application. Applications vary in descriptive terms, but the process is essentially the same. Clips are described and viewed in the list view window by title, length, and in and out points, among other items.

Footage then is assembled along a timeline in the assemble window. Each video and sound clip, graphic, and transition is added to the timeline in order by dragging the clip from the bin and placing it on the timeline. Clips may be trimmed and expanded, and transitions may be added along the timeline. After all clips and other materials have been assembled on the timeline, it may be previewed in real time to determine whether the edit is satisfactory. Because this is a virtual edit, no clips have actually been modified or lost. If the edit is satisfactory, the project is rendered, converting the virtual edit to an actual edit. The rendering process may take a few minutes or several days, depending on the length and complexity of the project.

Once rendered, the signal may be output to disc, tape, film, hard drive, or storage medium or converted to an analog signal for viewing and distribution. There is no technical difference between editing standard definition (SD) and high definition (HD), 4:3 and 16:9; it is just a matter of matching software and hardware. The original clips remain in the bin and may be used again in the same project or another project, or they may be stored for future use.

NONLINEAR EDITING PROCESS

Original video footage
shot on videotape

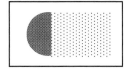

Videotape is compressed
and dubbed to a digital
medium

Video shots and audio
segments are chosen and
arranged in order by
dragging the pictures into
position on the
computer screen

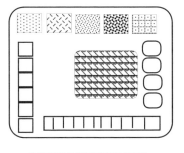

The completed production
may be stored on a hard disc,
floppy disc or converted
back to a videotape master

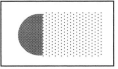

Creative Editing Methods

As in any creative, artistic field, there is an infinite number of methods for assembling a creative work. As a starting point, professionals consider three basic methods for assembling a videotape.

In the first method, a master wide shot that is laid down covers the entire sequence in one take. Then individual close-ups (CUs), cut-ins, cutaways, and cover shots, as well as medium shots and reversals at appropriate times in the tape, are added. Music and sound effects or voice-over narration then may be added to fit the edited video. With this method, the master shot determines the sequence length. For commercials and some news stories, a specific length must not be exceeded. An interview can be edited in this way, as can a demonstration or a musical sequence. The disadvantage is that you are tied to the master shot. If a CU does not match the same line or action in the master shot, the CU cannot be used because continuity will be lost.

The second method requires editing each shot in sequence. Cover shots are added to smooth transitions and avoid jump cuts. This method requires an editor with considerable skill and knowledge of the production and the available raw footage. Music and sound effects may be added during editing or after all of the video has been assembled.

In the third method, the audio is prerecorded by laying down the main audio track first. In a narration-based production, the narration is the main audio track. Shots are then recorded to match the narration. Music and sound effects may be added last. An alternative method, often used with music videos, is to lay down the music first, then record the shots of the musician lip-syncing. Additional dramatic or illustrative shots are added at appropriate times during the musical number. Additional sound (e.g., sound effects, music) may be mixed with the main audio track, or the second audio track can be used for the music and sound effects.

In reality, most editors use a combination of all three methods, depending on the needs of the production during that particular sequence. If the master tape is to be duplicated or released on CD or digital video disc (DVD), then you must write specific and precise instructions according to the recommendations of the duplicating company.

Your final duties as an editor include properly labeling all of the master and raw footage stock and computer discs. The discs, footage, and the boxes they are stored in must be labeled. All paper records—shooting and editing logs, director's and producer's instructions, and bookkeeping forms and records required by the accounting department—must be filled out and properly filed. Your work as an editor ends as it began, dealing with a pile of paperwork in order to perform your job more efficiently.

176

EDITING METHODS

Master Shot and CUs

Master Shot

Cutaway   CU

Master shot with CUs inserted at appropriate times

Shot Sequencing

Shot 1	Shot 2	Shot 3	Shot 4	Shot 5	Shot 6	

Individual shots assembled one after another

Final Video Edited to Audio

Audio recorded first

Shot 1	Shot 2	Shot 3	Shot 4	Shot 5	Shot 6

Video edited to match audio

177

Conclusion

As it is now obvious from the reading of this text, there is as much paperwork in media production as there is in any other single activity. The actual shooting of the production constitutes a minimum amount of the total time, although usually a maximum of the total physical effort, that goes into the production.

The critical stages occur during the preproduction and editing processes. If a production is not clearly and carefully planned before shooting starts, no amount of creative or physical effort will save the production. By the same token, if the shooting is not specifically planned with the editing process in mind, no amount of effort in the editing suite will salvage the production. These cautions apply to digital productions as much as to analog productions. The amazing capabilities of digital equipment will not be utilized if those capabilities are not properly planned for during the preproduction stages.

Also obvious is that there are few differences in electronic field production between analog and digital formats. Lighting, optics, audio, writing, composition and shooting, and basic editing all share the same techniques. Digital production from camera to final edited format will become the preferred medium, but all signals start and end as an analog signal.

My best advice is to plan for the worst and shoot for the best.

Further Reading

Alberstat, Philip. *Independent Producer's Guide to Film & Television Contracts*. Boston: Focal Press, 1999.

Alten, Stanley R. *Audio in Media*. 7th ed. Belmont, CA: Wadsworth Publishing, 2005.

Amyes, Tim. *Audio Post Production in Video & Film*. 2nd ed. Boston: Focal Press, 1999.

Anderson, Gary. *Video Editing and Post Production: A Professional Guide*. 4th ed. Boston: Focal Press, 1998.

Arntson, Amy E. *Graphic Design Basics*. 4th ed. Belmont, CA: Wadsworth Publishing, 2002.

Bayes, Steve. *The Avid Handbook*. 4th ed. Boston: Focal Press, 2003.

Benedetti, Robert. *From Concept to Screen: An Overview of Film and Television Production*. Boston: Allyn & Bacon, 2002.

Bermingham, Alan. *Lighting for Television*. Boston: Focal Press, 2001.

Box, Harry C. *Set Lighting Technician's Handbook*. 3rd ed. Boston: Focal Press, 2003.

Browne, Steven E. *Videotape Editing*: *A Postproduction Primer*. 4th ed. Boston: Focal Press, 2001.

Burrows, Thomas D., Lynne S. Gross, James C. Foust, and Donald N. Wood. *Video Production: Disciplines and Techniques*. 8th ed. Boston: McGraw-Hill, 2001.

Compesi, Ronald J. *Video Field Production and Editing*. 6th ed. Boston: Allyn & Bacon, 2003.

DiZazzo, Ray. *Corporate Media Production*. 2nd ed. Boston: Focal Press, 2004.

Eargle, John. *The Microphone Book*. Boston: Focal Press, 2001.

Favre, Jon. *Shooting Digital Video*. Boston: Focal Press, 2001.

Feldman, Tony. *An Introduction to Digital Media*. New York: Routledge, 1997.

Ferrara, Serena. *Steadicam: Techniques and Aesthetics*. Boston: Focal Press, 2001.

Fowler, Jaime. *Editing Digital Film: Integrating Final Cut, Avid, and Media 100*. Boston: Focal Press, 2001.

Friedmann, Anthony. *Writing for Visual Media*. Boston: Focal Press, 2001.

Gloman, Chuck, and Tom LeTourneau. *Placing of Shadows: Lighting Techniques for Video Production*. 2nd ed. Boston: Focal Press, 2000.

Grant, August E., and Jennifer N. Meadow. *Communication Technology Update*. 9th ed. Boston: Focal Press, 2004.

Grant, Tony. *Audio for Single Camera Operation*. Boston: Focal Press, 2003.

Gross, Lynne S., and Larry Ward. *Digital Moviemaking*. 5th ed. Belmont, CA: Wadsworth Publishing, 2004.

Hartwig, Robert L. *Basic TV Technology: Digital and Analog*. 3rd ed. Boston: Focal Press, 2000.

Hilliard, Robert L. *Writing for Television, Radio, and New Media*. 8th ed. Belmont, CA: Wadsworth Publishing, 2003.

Holman, Tomlinson. *Sound for Film and Television*. 2nd ed. Boston: Focal Press, 2001.

Jackman, John. *Lighting for Digital Video and Television*. San Francisco: CMP Books, 2002.

Kindem, Gorham, and Robert Musburger. *Introduction to Media Production: The Path to Digital*. 3rd ed. Boston: Focal Press, 2005.

Maes, Jan, and Mars Vecommen. *Digital Audio Technology, CD, MiniDisc, SACD, DVDA, MP3*. 4th ed. Boston: Focal Press, 2001.

Miller, Pat P. *Script Supervising and Film Continuity*. 3rd ed. Boston: Focal Press, 1999.

Millerson, Gerald. *Television Production*. 13th ed. Boston: Focal Press, 1999.

Rabiger, Michael. *Directing the Documentary*. 4th ed. Boston: Focal Press, 2004.

Roberts-Breslin, Jan. *Making Media: Foundations of Sound and Image*. Boston: Focal Press, 2003.

Rosenthal, Alan. *Writing, Directing, and Producing Documentaries*. 3rd ed. Carbondale, IL: Southern Illinois University Press, 1996.

Shook, Frederick. *Television Field Production and Reporting*. 3rd ed. Boston: Allyn & Bacon, 2000.

Sterling, Christopher, ed. *Focal Encyclopedia of Electronic Media*. CD-ROM. Boston: Focal Press, 1998.

Tolputt, Bob. *DV Filmmaking*. Boston: Focal Press, 2001.

Watkinson, John. *The Art of Digital Audio*. Boston: Focal Press, 2000.

Watkinson, John. *The Art of Digital Video*. 3rd ed. Boston: Focal Press, 2000.

Wiese, Michael, and Deke Simon. *Film and Video Budgets*. 3rd ed. Boston: Focal Press, 2001.

Zettl, Herbert. *Television Production Handbook*. 8th ed. Belmont, CA: Wadsworth Publishing, 2003.

Zettl, Herbert. *Video Lab*. 3rd ed. Belmont, CA: Wadsworth Publishing, 2004.

Zettl, Herbert. *Video Basics 2*. 4th ed. Belmont, CA: Wadsworth Publishing, 2004.

Zettl, Herbert. *Sight-Sound-Motion*. 4th ed. Belmont, CA: Wadsworth Publishing, 2005.

Glossary

A/B ROLL Editing process using two separate rolls (cassettes or reels) of tape. Each cassette contains alternate shots of the sequence, enabling the editor to use transitions other than straight cuts between shots.

ABSTRACT One of three basic media aesthetic choices. Abstract goes beyond realism, as seen in the way some music videos and science fiction dramas stretch the audience's imagination and sense of reality.

ADDITIVE The colors used in mixing light and on which both film and video signals are based: red, blue, and green.

ADVANCED TELEVISION SYSTEMS COMMITTEE (ATSC) An American professional group formed to set standards for television broadcasting beyond analog National Television Standards Committee, including high-definition and digital television standards.

AESTHETIC ASPECT One of two choices that need to be made during any media session. Aesthetic covers the creative, artistic values; the other consideration is the practical aspect.

AMBIENT Prevailing environment; in audio, the background noise present at a location.

AMPLITUDE The instantaneous value of a signal; the electronic equivalent of level or loudness in audio.

ANALOG Electronic signal that is constantly varying in some proportion to sound, light, or a radiofrequency.

APERTURE (IRIS) The size, measured in f-stops, of the lens opening.

APPLE BOX A series of various sized boxes used to stand on or to carry production items. It is manufactured in standard sizes with holes on two sides to ease carrying them about the set or location.

ASA EXPOSURE INDEX Numerical system that refers to the ability of a film stock to react to light. It is set by the American National Standards Institute.

ASPECT RATIO The measurement of width to height of the visual frame: 4:3 in National Television Standards Committee; 16:9 in high-definition television.

ASSEMBLE EDIT Sequential arranging of shots in a linear manner. It can be accomplished on raw tape without previously recording a control track.

ATSC-DTV (ADVANCED TELEVISION SYSTEMS COMMITTEE–DIGITAL TELEVISION) The digital video broadcast standard set by the U.S. Federal Communications Commission.

ATTENUATE   To decrease the level of an electronic signal.

AUDIO   The sound portion of the videotape. Frequencies within the normal hearing range of humans.

AURAL   Having to do with sound or audio.

AUTOMATIC GAIN CONTROL (AGC)   Circuit that maintains the audio or video gain within a certain range. It prevents overdriving circuits, which causes distortion, but can increase signal-to-noise ratio.

AUTOMATIC LEVEL CONTROL (ALC)   Circuit that maintains set levels at the output of an audio compressor to set the proper level for the next stage.

AVAILABLE LIGHT   Illumination existing at a location.

BACK FOCUS   The distance the lens must be mounted from the focal point for maximum focus.

BACKLIGHT   Light placed behind the subject, opposite the camera; it is usually mounted fairly high and is controlled with barn doors to prevent light from shining directly into the camera lens.

BALANCED LINE   An audio cable constructed with two conductors and a shield designed to provide the best protection from outside interference.

BARN DOOR   Movable metal flap attached to lighting fixtures to allow control over the area covered by the light from that lamp.

BARREL   A cable adapter designed to connect two cables ending in similar plugs.

BARS/GAIN ROLL   A switch that allows the camera operator to record color bars or change the gain setting of the internal video amplifier.

BASE LIGHT   The minimum amount of light required to provide an acceptable picture.

BASIC THREE-POINT LIGHTING   Lighting designed to satisfy the need for basic lighting to create an image and provide a realistic setting for a scene. This design derives its name from the three lighting instruments used to achieve satisfactory levels and appearance: key lights, fill lights, and backlights.

BASS   The low end of the audio spectrum.

BEL   Basic unit of audio measurement. It is usually too large for normal usage; therefore, decibels $\frac{1}{10}$ bel) commonly are used instead.

BETACAM   A $\frac{1}{2}$-inch professional videotape format developed by Sony specifically for use in a camcorder. Betacam has replaced $\frac{3}{4}$-inch U-matic as the predominant news gathering video format. Currently, it has been upgraded to BetaSP and Digital Beta.

BIDIRECTIONAL   Microphone that picks up sound from the front and back but rejects most sound from the sides. The pickup pattern appears in the shape of a figure eight.

BIT   The smallest digital measurement: 8 bits = 1 byte.

BLACK BURST   A composite video signal including synchronous and color signals, but the video level is at black, or minimum.

BLACK LEVEL   The normal level for pedestal or video black in a video signal. See also *Setup*.

BLEED   Space beyond the critical or essential area that may be seen on some television receivers but not on others.

BLOOM   The effect seen when a video signal exceeds the capabilities of the system: white areas bleed into darker areas.

BNC   A type of twist-lock video connector; currently, it is the most common type for professional equipment.

BODY MICROPHONE   A microphone concealed or hung directly on the body of the performer, sometimes called a lapelor lavalier microphone.

BODY MOUNT   A method of holding and controlling a camera without the use of a tripod or other fixed mounting. The most common type is the Steadicam, which uses a series of gyroscopes, springs, and counter weights.

BOOM   Movable arm from which a microphone or camera may be suspended to allow for movement to follow the action.

BOOST   To increase the level of an electronic signal.

BRIGHTNESS   The luminance value of a video picture.

BROAD   A type of open-faced fill light, usually rectangular in shape.

BUBBLE   Leveling device mounted on a tripod pan head consisting of a tube containing liquid with a bubble of air trapped inside. Centering the bubble on a circle or cross-hair indicates that the pan head is level.

BURN   A condition caused by exposing camera tubes to excessive light levels. An image is retained on the face of the tube that is the negative of the original subject.

BUST SHOT   The composition of framing a human from slightly above the waist to the top of the head.

BYTE   A measurable number of bits treated as a unit. Also, a convenient measurement of digital memory.

C FORMAT   One of three 1-inch helical videotape formats specified by the SMPTE. C format was the analog production standard for studios in the United States before digital video became practical.

CAMCORDER   Camera–recorder combination. Designed originally for news coverage but is now becoming popular for EFP and other field productions.

CARDIOID MICROPHONE   Specialized unidirectional microphone with a heart-shaped pickup pattern.

CASE   Style of letters. Uppercase letters are capital letters; lowercase letters are small letters.

CASSETTE   Prepackaged container of either audio tape or videotape containing a specific length of tape stock, a feed reel, and a take-up reel. U-matic, BetaSP, VHS, and Hi-8 Systems all use incompatible videocassettes.

CATHODE RAY TUBE (CRT)   The large picture tube used as video monitors and television receivers.

CENTRAL PROCESSING UNIT (CPU)   The main control and operating circuits of a computer.

CHARACTER GENERATOR (CG)   Computerized electronic typewriter designed to create titles or any other alphanumeric graphics for use in video.

CHARGE-COUPLED DEVICE (CCD)   A solid-state element designed to convert light to electronics; it replaces the pickup tubes in video cameras.

CHIAROSCURO LIGHTING   Lighting accomplished with high-contrast areas and heavy shadows.

CHIP   Semiconductor integrated circuit. Depending on its design, a chip can replace tubes, resistors, and other electronic components. The most important development for EFP is the light-sensitive chip that replaces the camera tube.

CHROMINANCE   The portion of the video signal controlling color.

CINEMATOGRAPHER   Its narrowest definition is the operator or supervisor of a motion picture camera. Over the years, the job description of a cinematographer often has come to include the field of operating a video camera.

CLOSE-UP (CU)   The second tightest shot in a sequence. Camera framing showing intimate detail; often a tight head shot.

CLOSURE   Psychological perceptual activity that fills in gaps in the visual field.

COLOR BARS   Electronically generated pattern of precisely specified colors for use in standardizing the operation of video equipment.

COLOR TEMPERATURE   See *Kelvin Temperature.*

COLOR TEMPERATURE CONTROL   A series of filters enabling the camera operator to compensate for the variations in Kelvin temperature of the location.

COMPACT DISC READ-ONLY MEMORY (CD-ROM)   A permanently recorded digital compact disc.

COMPRESSION   In the digitizing process, certain unnecessary or redundant portions of the signal are not digitized, which saves precious storage memory.

184

CONDENSER MICROPHONE Transducer that converts sound waves by conductive principle. It requires a built-in amplifier and a power source. Also called electrostatic or capacitor mic.

CONNECTOR PANEL Usually a section on the rear of a piece of equipment where the jacks are located.

CONTINUITY 1. A depiction of continuous action, location, direction, or time. 2. Script written for spots—commercials, public service announcements, or promotional announcements.

CONTINUITY ASSISTANT (CA) The member of the crew who follows the shooting script, keeps track of the logs, and checks to ensure that the sequence between shots will match later in the editing process.

CONTRAST RANGE Ability of a camera to distinguish between shades of reflected black and white light: 30:1 in television, 100:1 in film, and 1,000:1 with the human eye.

CONTRAST RATIO The mathematical comparison of the measured light value reflected from the brightest part of the picture with detail and the darkest part of the picture with detail.

CONTROL TRACK Synchronizing signal recorded onto a videotape to align the heads for proper playback.

CONTROLLER A specialized computer designed to accurately maintain control over a series of videotape decks during the editing process.

COOKIE See *Cukaloris*.

COPY The words on a script.

COUNTER A meter designed to indicate either a position on a reel of tape or the amount of tape already used. It may be calibrated in revolutions, feet, meters, or time.

COVER SHOT Any one of several shots, usually close-ups, designed to give the editor a means of preserving continuity. See also *Cutaways* and *Cut-ins*.

CRAB DOLLY A small platform large enough for a tripod and camera operator. It usually has four wheels; two are designed to provide a way to steer the dolly. It is usually pushed by a crew member and sometimes is set on tracks for a tracking shot.

CRANES One of the support systems used for single-camera production. Cranes are designed to permit the camera to be raised and lowered over a wide range, as well as to swing back and forth 360 degrees when necessary.

CRITICAL AREA (ESSENTIAL AREA) Space occupying approximately 80% of the center of the video frame. This area is seen with relative surety by the majority of the television receivers viewing

185

that particular program. The 10% border outside of the critical area may not be seen by many receivers.

CROSS-KEY LIGHT A single instrument used to provide key light for one subject and, at the same time, fill light for another subject.

CUE 1. Signal to start talking, moving, or whatever the script calls for. 2. To ready material to be played back or edited by running and stopping a tape, film, or record, among other items, at a specified spot.

CUKALORIS A pattern inserted into an ellipsoidal spotlight to throw a mottled design onto the background. Also known as cookie.

CUT (TAKE) 1. Cue to stop an action. 2. An instantaneous change in picture or sound. "Cut" is considered a film term, and "take" is considered a video term, but they have become interchangeable.

CUTAWAY Close-up shot of an image related to, but not visible in, the wider shot immediately preceding or following it.

CUT-IN Close-up shot of an image visible in the wider shot immediately preceding or following it.

CYCLE Time or distance between peaks of an alternating voltage. It is measured in hertz (Hz).

DECIBEL (DB) Logarithmic unit of loudness. A dB is $\frac{1}{10}$ of the original unit, the bel.

DECK In media, a machine that plays and/or records audio or video signals.

DEMODULATOR Separates audio and video signals in a cable.

DEPTH OF FIELD (DOF) The range of distances from the camera within which subjects remain in acceptable focus.

DIALOGUE Speech between performers, usually seen on camera.

DICHROIC Filters designed to reflect certain colors of light and to pass other colors.

DIGITAL Binary-based, constant-amplitude signals varying in time. Professional video signal recording without noise or distortion.

DIGITAL CINEMA (DC) Formerly known as Electronic Cinema. A video format designed to rival the quality of 35-mm film.

DIGITAL SUBSCRIBER LINE (DSL) A standard telephone line set up to carry broadband signals.

DIGITAL VIDEO CAMERA (DVC) A ½-inch digital videotape format. Various versions range from DVCam (prosumer level) to DVCPro (professional broadcast level) to PVCProHD (professional high-definition level). There is some compatibility among levels and manufacturers.

DIN (DEUTSCHE INDUSTRIE NORMEN) The German standards organization. DIN usually refers to a type of plug or jack.

186

DIRECTOR   Commands the creative aspects of a production. In the field, the director makes creative decisions. In the studio, the director calls the shots on live productions. In the editing room, the director provides opinions.

DISC   A digital recording medium. It may be either magnetic or optical. Examples range from the 3.5-inch floppy disc to 5-inch CD-ROMs and DVDs to large hard drives.

DISSOLVE   Transition of one image fading into and replacing another. If stopped at the midpoint, it is a superimposition. Also called a lap.

DISTORTION   An undesirable change in a signal.

DISTRIBUTION AMPLIFIER (DA)   Electronic amplifier designed to feed one signal (audio, video, or pulses) to several different destinations.

DOLLY   1. Three- or four-wheeled device that serves as a movable camera mount. 2. Movement in toward a subject (dolly in) or back away from a subject (dolly out).

DOWNLINK   Transmission path from a satellite to a ground station. Sometimes used to describe the ground station capable of receiving a satellite signal. See also *Uplink*.

DRAG   The back pressure designed to make panning and tilting a camera head smooth and controlled. The drag can be created by friction, fluid, spring, or geared mechanisms.

DUAL-COLUMN FORMAT   A scripting format used primarily for live or tape-to-live video and television productions. It has been developed over the years from radio and audio/video formats. All video and movement instructions are located in the left-hand column, whereas audio instructions are in the right-hand column.

DUB   1. Copying a recorded signal from one medium to another. 2. Replacing or adding voice to a preexisting recording; now called automatic dialogue replacement (ADR).

DVB-T (DIGITAL VIDEO BROADCAST-TERRESTRIAL)   The high-definition technical standard developed by European on-air broadcasters.

DYNAMIC MICROPHONE   Transducer designed to convert sound to electronics by using an electromagnetic coil attached to a light-weight diaphragm.

DYNAMIC RANGE   Loudness range from the softest to the loudest that can be reproduced by any system without creating distortion.

DYNAMICS   The difference between the loudest and the quietest passage.

EDGE ATTRACTION THEORY   When an object appears to move toward the edge, even if it remains stationary in the frame.

187

EDGE BLEED AREA The 10% border around a frame that may be seen by some viewers.

EDIT DECISION LIST (EDL) List of precise locations of edit points. It may be generated manually or by a computer.

EDITOR Tape or film specialist charged with assembling stories from footage and recordings to create the final production.

EIAJ (ELECTRONIC INDUSTRIES ASSOCIATION OF JAPAN) Organization that sets standards for Japan. At one time, EIAJ referred to a specific ½-inch open-reel videotape system.

ELECTRET A small condenser microphone often used as a lavalier or microphone built-in to equipment.

ELECTRONIC FIELD PRODUCTION (EFP) Process of researching, shooting, and editing materials to be used in non-news productions.

ELECTRONIC NEWS GATHERING (ENG) Process of researching, shooting, and editing materials to visually report on occurrences of interest using video cameras and electronic editing specifically for newscasts.

EQUALIZATION Process of compensating for required changes in frequency, level, or phase of an audio or video signal.

EXTERIOR (EXT) An outdoor setting or location.

EXTREME CLOSE-UP (ECU, ALSO XCU) The tightest framing of a shot in a sequence. It is usually reserved for an effect. A very close view of a product would be an ECU.

EXTREME WIDE SHOT (EWS, ALSO XWS) The widest shot of a sequence—for example, a shot from a blimp, an entire city block, or a football stadium.

F A type of connector for a cable intended to carry a modulated signal or signals. See also *Radiofrequency (RF)*.

FACILITIES Technical equipment, lights, cameras, microphones, and so on.

FACSIMILE (FAX) Transmission of information by an optical/electronic system through telephone lines.

FADE-IN/FADE-OUT A gradual change in signal, either from zero to maximum or maximum to zero. Can apply to either audio or video.

FAY A series of fixed-focus lamps mounted in a bank. A Fay has a color temperature of 5,400 K. See also *Par*.

FEDERAL COMMUNICATIONS COMMISSION (FCC) Federal agency charged with the supervision and regulation of all electronic communication media in the United States.

FIELD One-half of a complete interlaced television picture; 262.5 lines of the 525 NTSC system occurring once every ⅟₆₀ of a second. Two interlaced fields make a complete frame. One complete progressive video field may consist of from 360 to 1,040 lines in a single fame.

FIELD OF VIEW   The range of subjects and settings that a camera shows in a single shot.

FILL LIGHT   Soft, shadowless light used to reduce contrast and lighten shadow areas. It is usually placed on the opposite side of the camera from the key light and low enough to remove harsh shadows.

FILTER   A colored element placed in front of or behind a lens.

FIREWIRE (IEEE 1394)   A standard for transmission of data between digital equipment. A high-performance standard is becoming one of the preferred methods of moving data in the media production world. Also known as iSync.

FISH POLE   Handheld expandable microphone boom.

FIXED-FOCUS INSTRUMENTS   One of the three basic types of field lighting instruments. Fixed-focus instruments are designed around a lamp similar to an auto headlight.

FLAG   An opaque piece of material hung between a light and the subject or set to control light or throw a shadow.

FLASH FRAME   An unwanted frame between two edited shots.

FLOODLIGHT   A nonlensed instrument that provides soft, diffused light.

FLUORESCENT LIGHT   Gas-filled tube that emits light when an electrical current ionizes the gas. It does not emit light of a specific Kelvin temperature but is bluish green in color.

FLYING ERASE HEAD   Erase head mounted on the rotating head mount of a helical recorder. It is designed to allow precise editing of the video signal without losing synchronization between shots.

FOCAL LENGTH   Theoretical distance from the optical center of the lens to the focal plane. It is determined by the size of the image surface, the angle of view, depth of field, and image size.

FOCAL POINT   The position behind the lens where the image is concentrated.

FOCUS   The ability of a lens to create the sharpest image of a subject.

FOCUSING SPOTLIGHTS   One of the three basic types of field lighting instruments. Focusing spotlights are either open faced without a lens or have a Fresnel or plano-convex lens. Focusing spotlights are essential for critical creative lighting.

FOLEY SESSION   A studio designed to create sounds in postproduction. It is named for Jack Foley, an early sound operator in film.

FOOT CANDLE   Older measurement of illumination. Originally, the amount of light from one candle, falling on an area of 1 square foot, 1 foot from the candle.

FORMAT, VIDEOTAPE   Specifications of a specific type of videotape. There are approximately 23 different formats currently in use.

FRAME   1. Complete video picture, made up of two 262.5-line, interlaced, scanned fields. There are 30 frames per second in the NTSC system. 2. In HDTV, there are 360 to 1,040 lines in the progressive system at a rate of 24 to 60 frames per second. 3. The outline of the available area in which to compose a video picture. Currently, the NTSC standard is a frame 3 units high by 4 units wide; the HDTV standard is 9 units high by 16 units wide.

FREEZE FRAME   Stopping a single frame within a moving sequence.

FREQUENCY   The number of complete cycles an electrical signal makes in 1 second. It is measured in hertz (Hz).

FREQUENCY RESPONSE   A measurement of the ability of a piece of equipment to reproduce a signal of varying frequencies.

FRESNEL   A spotlight equipped with a stepped lens that easily controls and concentrates light.

FRONT FOCUS   Creating the sharpest picture by adjusting the lens.

F-STOP   A measurement of the size of an opening that allows light to pass through an iris or aperture.

FUSE BOX (CIRCUIT BREAKER BOX)   The location of alternating current power distribution with individual switches or fuses (in older locations), which protect each circuit from having too much current drawn from it.

GAFFER   Senior electrician on a crew.

GAIN   The amount of amplitude of an electronic signal. It is usually measured in decibels (dB).

GAIN CONTROL   An electronic control in a camera; it is usually located internally.

GEN-LOCK   Abbreviation for synchronous generation locking. Electronically connecting all circuits together so that synchronization will remain stable.

GENRE   A type of programming (for example, western, comedy, or drama).

GIGAHERTZ   A measurement of frequency: 1 gigahertz = 1,000,000,000 hertz.

GIRAFFE   Small microphone boom mounted on a tripod on wheels; it is usually designed for limited microphone movement.

GOBO   1. In video, a set piece, such as a window, that allows a camera to shoot through it. 2. In audio, a movable sound reflector board. 3. In film, a movable freestanding pattern cutout similar to a cookie. 4. Onstage, the equivalent of a cookie.

190

GRAPHICS GENERATOR   A digital unit designed to create and combine pictures with type. It is sometimes called a paint box.

GRAPHIC WEIGHT (GRAPHIC FORCE)   The perceived value of any item within the picture frame.

GRAY SCALE   Multistep intensity scale for the evaluation of a picture. Generally, there are 10 steps between television white and television black.

GRIP   A stagehand/crew member who moves sets, props, and dollies, among other items. The head stagehand is the key grip.

GUN   A part of a picture and a camera tube that shoots a stream of electronics at the faceplate of the tube.

HAND PROPS   Items small enough to be picked up and handled; however, for the most part, they are items that need to be handled by the talent during the production.

HARD DRIVE   A magnetic disk drive designed to store large amounts of digital information. Most computers have at least one hard drive installed internally, but hard drives can also be connected externally to digital equipment.

HEAD   A pan head supports the camera and is designed to allow both horizontal and vertical movement of the camera.

HEAD SHOT   A composition of framing the person just above the shoulders to above the top of the head.

HELICAL   Videotape with multiple recording heads that record information in long, slanting tracks; each track records one field of information.

HELICAL RECORDING   See *Helical*.

HERTZ (Hz)   Measurement of frequency. Number of complete cycles completed in 1 second.

HI-8   Semiprofessional 8-mm videotape format developed by Sony for the prosumer market.

HIGH-DEFINITION TELEVISION (HDTV)   One of several subcategories of advanced television (ATV). Attempt at creating a video system nearly equal to 35-mm film in resolution and aspect ratio.

HIGH HAT   A minimal platform designed to mount a pan head, allowing for shots close to the ground, or to mount the camera on a car, boat, or airplane.

HIGH IMPEDANCE   A measurement of resistance to current flowing through a cable. High-impedance lines generally are designed to carry signals amplified to at least mid-level to prevent noise being added. Some microphones are rated as high impedance, but they must be connected to short cables to prevent picking up extraneous noise.

IDIOT CARDS   A prompting device made of large, bold keywords written on cards held next to the camera lens for the talent's benefit.

IMAGE ORTHICON (I-O)   An early video camera tube. The development of the I-O opened the way for reasonably mobile studio and remote cameras.

IMPEDANCE   Apparent alternating current resistance to current flowing in a circuit. It is measured in ohms.

INCANDESCENT LIGHT   Inert, gas-filled electric lamp emitting light and heat from a glowing filament. A typical lamp is the tungsten-halogen lamp used in most production instruments.

INCIDENT LIGHT   Illumination from a light source. It is measured in foot candles or lux by pointing the light meter at the light source.

INPUT   Signal entering a system or an electrical unit.

INSERT EDIT   Assembling a videotape production by adding video and audio signals to tape stock that already has had control track recorded on it. Insert edits also can be made over existing edited tape.

INTEGRATED SERVICE DIGITAL BROADCAST (ISDB)   The digital broadcast standard set for Japan.

INTERIOR (INT)   Setting or location inside of a building or structure.

INTERLACED SCANNING   The method of combining two fields of scan lines into one frame.

INTERNAL GAIN CONTROL   A potentiometer that allows continuous gain settings on a camera.

INTERVALOMETER   A control that sets the number of frames per second at which the recorder will operate. This compresses the action in any time elapsed required for the production.

INTRO   Abbreviation for introduction.

INVERSE SQUARE LAW   A mathematical analysis of changes in alternating energy. The amount of energy is inversely proportionate to the change in distance. The formula is easily applied to calculations of lighting and audio levels.

IRIS   See *Aperture*.

IRIS FADE-IN/FADE-OUT   An iris fade-in or fade-out is created by placing the iris control on manual and setting the iris opening stopped all the way down. With the tape rolling, the iris may be slowly opened up and brought to the proper setting, thus creating a fade-in. A fade-out is created by reversing the procedure: A scene is started with the tape rolling and the iris set properly. At the right moment, the iris is stopped down until the picture fades to black. Neither of these effects works well unless the light level is low enough that the iris is nearly wide open at the proper setting.

IRIS INST. CONTROL   A camera control designed so that you can zoom in on the surface that is reflecting the average amount of light for that scene, such as the face of the subject. Press the iris inst. control, which locks the iris at that setting, and then zoom back and/or pan to whatever framing is needed or to the beginning of that scene.

IRIS MODE CONTROL   Allows you to choose between setting the iris manually or letting the camera's automatic iris circuits set the iris.

JACK   A cable connector mounted on equipment.

JARGON   Terminology and slang of a particular field.

JUMP CUT   Any one of several types of poor edits that either break continuity or may be disturbing to the audience.

KELVIN TEMPERATURE   Measurement of the relative color of light; indicated as degrees Kelvin. The greater the temperature, the bluer the light is; the lower the temperature, the redder the light is. Also known as color temperature.

KEY LIGHT   Apparent main source of light, usually from one bright light above and to one side of the camera.

KICKER   A light focused from the side of the subject or on a particular section of the set.

KILOHERTZ (kHz)   A measurement of alternating energy: 1,000 hertz.

LAG   That characteristic of a camera tube in which a picture trails its own images as the camera moves. Lag increases with the age of the tube.

LAPTOP   A portable computer designed small enough to fold and carry. It is also a term for laptop editor. A single-unit, portable, non-linear editor.

LAVALIER (LAV)   Microphone worn around the neck. It is also sometimes called a lapel microphone when clipped to a tie or to the front of the clothing.

LAYING DOWN CONTROL TRACK   The process of recording a synchronous signal. It requires a video signal and a set of synchronous signals, but no audio is needed. It usually records color bars or a video black signal.

LEAD ROOM   Extra space in front of any moving object in the camera frame.

LENS   Glass or plastic designed to focus and concentrate light on a surface to form an image.

LENS CAP   Opaque covering to slip over the end of a lens to protect the surface from damage and to protect the image device from excessive light.

LEVEL   Relative amplitude or intensity. It is used to indicate light audio, video, and other electronic signals.

LIGHT-EMITTING DIODE (LED)   A solid-state component that emits light when a small voltage is applied. It is useful as a level or operating condition indicator.

LIGHT METER (EXPOSURE METER)   Instrument used to measure the intensity of light. It may be calculated in foot candles, lux, or f-stops.

LIGHTING RATIO   A numerical value comparing the amount of incident light provided by the fill lights alone against the amount of incident light provided by the combination of key plus fill light. The standard ratio is 2:1.

LINE LEVEL   Signal amplified enough to feed down a line without fear of degradation. A microphone level is lower than line level; a speaker level is greater than line level.

LINEAR   In a straight line.

LIQUID CRYSTAL DISPLAY (LCD)   1. A flat-screen video monitor. 2. A source of flat, even light balanced to daylight.

LOCAL AREA NETWORK (LAN)   A set of wires designed to carry digital signals between several peripherals or computers.

LOCATION   Area or site of a production. It usually refers to sites away from studios.

LOG   Listing of shots as they are recorded on tape.

LONGITUDINAL   Lengthwise. In media, it refers to the method of recording audio and control track signals.

LOOPING   The process of rerecording audio during postproduction. It is now called automatic dialogue replacement (ADR).

LOUDNESS   Perceived intensity of audio, depending on the intensity and saturation of the sound, as well as the sensitivity of the listener to a range of frequencies.

LOW IMPEDANCE   A measurement of resistance to current flow. Low-impedance circuits often are at a low level. High-quality microphone lines are low impedance with two conductors and a shield to prevent noise entering the circuit.

LUMINANCE   The brightness component of a video signal.

LUX   European measurement of light intensity. There are approximately 10 lux per one 1-foot candle.

MASTER SHOT   Extended wide shot establishing the scene and often running the entire length of the sequence. It is intended to be broken down in the editing process.

MATTE BOX   A mounting mechanism on the front of a lens designed to hold filters, sun shades, or other accessories used in electronic cinematography.

MEDIUM CLOSE-UP (MCU)   Relative average framing for a shot, often framed from the waist up.

MEDIUM SHOT (MS)   Wider than an MCU, often framed head to toe.

MEMORY CARD   A thin combination of solid-state circuits designed to store digital signals.

MENUS   A series of operational options that can be read in the viewfinder of a camera or on the face of a recorder. The options may be modified by watching the menus while adjusting the equipment.

METAL OXIDE SEMICONDUCTOR (MOS)   1. A type of solid-state element designed to convert light to electronics; it replaces the pickup tube in video cameras. 2. A film term indicating a shot was recorded silent, or as the early German film directors said, "Mit (with) out sound."

M FORMAT (M-II, RECAM)   Professional ½-inch format previously manufactured by Panasonic. It was originally sold by RCA as Recam, and then upgraded to M-II. It has been replaced by Panasonic digital formats.

MICROWAVE   High-frequency carrier for both audio and video signals. Operates only on a line-of-sight path.

MINI-PLUG (⅛-INCH)   Audio connector designed for small equipment. Scaled-down version of ¼-inch phone plug.

MIXED LIGHTING   A set lit with light of various Kelvin temperatures.

MIXER   A piece of electronic equipment designed to combine several signals. It usually refers to an audio board or console.

MODULATOR   An electronic component designed to impress one signal on another, usually of a higher frequency.

MONITOR   1. To listen to or watch audio tapes, videotapes, or off-air programs. 2. Device used to view video signals, much like a television receiver, but usually of much higher quality and generally with a radiofrequency section for off-air monitoring.

MORGUE   Library, reference files, and storage for used scripts, tapes, maps, and other reference material.

MOTION PICTURE EXPERTS GROUP (MPEG)   A series of compression standards used in digitizing visual media.

NAT SOUND   Ambient sound that exists on location and is recorded as a story happens. It is often used as background for a voice-over. It is sometimes called wild sound.

NATIONAL TELEVISION STANDARDS COMMITTEE (NTSC)   1. The organization charged with setting television standards in the United States in the early days of television. 2. The television standard currently in use in North America, much of South America, and Japan.

195

NEUTRAL   An aesthetic level without any specific genre or setting, often used for newscasts.

NEUTRAL DENSITY (ND)   A type of filter that decreases light passage without changing the color value of the light.

NOISE   Any undesirable additions to a signal.

NONLINEAR   The storage and editing of video and audio digital signals. It is comparable with film editing in that edits can be made in any order without disturbing previously edited sequences; it is also nondestructive in that the original footage is not handled during the editing process.

NOSE ROOM   The extra space allowed for in front of the face when framing the human head if facing in a specific direction.

NOTAN   A lighting style similar to Japanese watercolors—high-key, few shadows, and evenly lit.

OFF-LINE   Using the lowest-quality and lowest-cost editing system suitable for a particular project.

OMNIDIRECTIONAL   Microphone pickup pattern that covers 360 degrees around the microphone.

ONLINE   Using the highest quality and highest cost editing system suitable for a particular project.

OPEN UP   The process of increasing aperture size in a lens, whereas the f-stop number decreases in size.

OPERATOR   Person whose main responsibility is to operate equipment, in contrast with technicians, whose main responsibility is to install, repair, and maintain equipment; and engineers, whose main responsibility it is to research, design, and construct equipment.

OPTICS/OPTICAL   Having to do with lenses or other light-carrying components of a video or film system.

OSCILLOSCOPE   Test equipment used to visualize a time factor system, such as a video signal. It shows a technician what the picture looks like electronically. It may also be used to analyze audio or other signals.

OUTPUT   Signal leaving a system or electrical unit.

OVER-THE-SHOULDER (OS)   A shot framed with two subjects: one facing the camera and the other with his or her back to the camera so only a portion of the shoulder is visible; for example, a typical news interview shot in which part of the interviewer's shoulder appears in the foreground and the person being interviewed faces the camera.

PAN   Horizontal movement of a camera; short for panorama.

PAN HEAD   Mechanism designed to firmly hold a camera on the top of a tripod, pedestal, or boom while allowing for smooth, easily controlled movement of the camera horizontally (pan) and

196

vertically (tilt). It may be mechanical, fluid, geared, or counter-balanced.

PAR   A series of fixed-focus lamps mounted in a bank. A par has a color temperature of 3,200 K. See also *Fay.*

PARABOLIC MICROPHONE   Focused, concave, reflective, bowl-shaped surface with a microphone mounted at the point of focus. It is used to pick up specific sounds at a distance; commonly used during sporting events.

PEDESTAL   1. Electronic calibration between blanking and black level. 2. Hydraulic, compressed air, or counterbalanced studio camera mount; designed to permit the camera to be raised straight up or down effortlessly and smoothly.

PEDESTAL CONTROL   Changes the black level or contrast of the picture.

PERAMBULATOR   A large, wheeled, platform-mounted boom that a microphone boom operator rides. Capable of swinging a microphone over a large area.

PERIPHERAL   Accessories connected to digital equipment, for example, printers, decks, and hard drives.

PHANTOM POWER   The 48 volts required by condenser microphone (mic) preamplifiers located in the mic. If the mic does not carry its own battery power, phantom power may be supplied through the mic line by the mixer or recorder.

PHASE   The relationship of two signals differing in time but on a common path.

PHASE ALTERNATIVE LINE (PAL)   A television system developed in Germany but used throughout the world in English-speaking countries or countries with ties to the United Kingdom that uses 625 lines and 25 frames, rather than the 525 lines and 60 frames used by the NTSC. It is used in many countries around the world.

PHOTOGRAPHER   Originally, a person taking still photographs. In some markets, the term *photographer* was applied to news cinematographers, and even today, the term sometimes is applied to videographers.

PITCH   Human perception of frequency.

PIXEL   A short version of "picture element." A single sample of digital color information.

PIXILATION   A process of removing a certain number of frames from a sequence so that the objects appear to be jumping about or suspended and moving in space.

PLASMA DISPLAY PANEL (PDP)   Flat-screen video monitor.

PLOSIVE SOUNDS   Sounds made by the human voice that tend to pop a microphone. Sounds beginning with the letters *p* and *b,* among others.

PLOT   A scale drawing of the location of a shoot.

PLUG   A connector on the end of a cable.

POINT OF VIEW (POV)   A camera angle giving the impression of the view of someone in the scene.

POWER SELECTOR SWITCH   A control on a camera or tape deck used to switch the power source from either a battery or external alternating current power.

PREAMPLIFIER (PREAMP)   Electronic circuit designed to amplify a weak signal to a usable level without introducing noise or distortion.

PRIME LENS   A fixed focal length lens.

PRISM   A glass or plastic block shaped to transmit or reflect light into different paths.

PRODUCER   Person in charge of a specific program.

PROGRESSIVE SCANNING   A video frame constructed of a series of lines continuously forming a single frame before starting another scan sequence.

PROMPTER   Device used to provide the talent with the copy as they perform on camera. It can be handheld copy beside the camera or a signal fed to a monitor mounted with mirrors to project the copy in front of the camera lens so that the anchor can look directly into the camera. This signal may be coming from a black-and-white camera shooting pages of the script or from a signal fed directly from a computer.

PROPOSAL   A concise summary of a project intended as a sales tool to accurately describe a production and to sell a sponsor on funding.

PROSUMER   A category of producer and equipment that falls below that of professional quality but is of higher quality than consumer products.

PUBLIC ADDRESS (PA)   Sound-reinforcing system designed to feed sound to an audience assembled in a large room.

PULLING FOCUS   The process of changing focus in the middle of a shot. It is also known as rack or rolling focus.

PULSE CODE MODULATION (PCM)   A digital recording system based on sampling an analog signal at regular intervals (usually audio).

QUADRAPLEX (QUAD)   The first practical professional videotape format. Quadraplex used 2-inch tape pulled across four heads to achieve a high-quality signal. It is no longer manufactured.

198

QUANTIZATION   The measurement of a signal indicating the number of discrete levels of analog measured in the conversion process to a digital signal.

QUARTER-INCH (¼-INCH) PLUG (PHONE)   Audio connector used for many years for high-impedance signals. It is still used in some consumer equipment and patch panels.

QUARTZ-HALOGEN   A lamp designed to provide a fixed color temperature of 3,200 K.

RACK FOCUS   Changing focus in the middle of a shot. See also *Pulling Focus*.

RADIOFREQUENCY (RF)   1. Those frequencies above the aural frequencies. 2. A type of plug attached to a cable designed to carry a modulated signal. It is also called F plug.

RASTER   The complete sequence of lines that make up the field of lines creating a video picture.

RCA   The U.S. corporation that promoted the NTSC video system, the developer of many early television inventions, and the original owner of NBC radio and television.

RCA PLUG (PHONO)   Audio and video connector designed originally for use only with the RCA-45 rpm record player. Currently used as a consumer audio and video connector. Some professional equipment uses this plug for line level audio. It should not be confused with the (phone ¼-inch) plug.

REALISTIC   An aesthetic value of production creating as lifelike a setting as possible.

RECORDER DECK   In a linear editing system, the tape deck that records the final edited sequence. See also *Editor*.

REFLECTANCE VALUES   The amount of light reflected from the brightest and darkest objects in the picture used to determine contrast ratio.

REFLECTED LIGHT   Illumination entering a lens reflected from an object. It is measured with a reflected light meter pointing at the object from the camera.

REFLECTORS   Large foam boards covered on one side with a variety of surfaces—plain white, colored, or textured. They are used to throw a soft fill light into areas not easily reached with instruments or to provide light when an instrument is not available or would cast an additional shadow.

REGISTRATION   The alignment of either electronic or physical components of a system. It is especially important in tube cameras.

RELEASE   1. Legal document allowing the videographer to use the image and/or voice of a subject. 2. Public relations copy.

199

RESOLUTION   Ability of a system to reproduce fine detail. In video, there are limits imposed by the NTSC video system.

RETURN VIDEO OR VIDEOTAPE RECORDER RETURN (VTR) CONTROL   A button on the camera that, when pressed, feeds the picture being played back from the tape deck into the viewfinder, allowing the videographer to observe the images already recorded.

REVERSING POLARITY   Electronically changing video light values from dark to bright and colors to their opposites.

RIBBON MICROPHONE   A transducer using a thin gold or silver corrugated ribbon suspended between the poles of a magnet to create an electrical output.

RIDING GAIN   The manual process of maintaining specific levels of electronic signals.

ROLL   The command given by the director to start tape or the film camera recording.

ROLLING OR PULLING FOCUS   Changing focus on a camera while recording.

RULE OF THIRDS   The composition and framing theory that the visual frame may be split into nine sections by the intersection of two vertical lines and two horizontal lines, each one third of the way into the frame.

SAMPLING   In the process of converting an analog signal to digital, the number of times per second the signal is measured to determine the equivalent digital signal.

SATELLITE   Geostationary orbiting space platform with transponders to pick up signals from Earth and retransmit the signals back down to Earth in a pattern, called a footprint, that covers a large area of the earth.

SATURATION   Intensity of a signal, either audio or video, but especially used as the third of three characteristics of a color video signal.

SCAN AREA   The portion of the subject that the camera converts into an electronic signal.

SCENE   A series of related shots, usually in the same time and location.

SCENE SCRIPT   A full script without individual shots indicated.

SCRIM   A metallic or fabric filter placed over a lighting instrument to diffuse and soften the light.

SCRIPT   Complete manuscript of all audio copy and video instructions of a program.

SEPARATE VIDEO HOME SYSTEM (S-VHS) PLUG   A plug that carries video signals split into two separate signals, Y and C, for higher-quality transmission of video than standard VHS.

200

SEQUENCE   Individual shots edited into scenes, and individual scenes edited together to make a story.

SEQUENTIAL COLOR WITH MEMORY (SECAM)   The color television system developed by the French. It is currently being phased out, although some third world countries may still be using it for black-and-white TV.

SET   The physical space within a studio for the production of a visual scene.

SET DESIGN   The process of creating on paper the environment for a visual production.

SET LIGHT   A lamp focusing on the area behind the talent or objects to provide a pattern on the background or to wipe out unwanted shadows.

SET PIECES   A type of dressing for a set: furniture, wall hangings, or objects too large or fixed in place to be handled by the talent.

SET UP   The assembly of equipment and people in preparation for rehearsing a production.

SETUP   Same as pedestal and black level; electronic calibration between blanking and black level.

SHOOTING LIST (SHOT SHEET)   A listing of all shots in the order they are to be made, regardless of their order in the script.

SHOOTING SCRIPT   A script complete in all details, including specific shot descriptions.

SHOT   One continuous roll of the recorder; the smallest unit of a script.

SHOTGUN   Ultra-unidirectional microphone designed to pick up sound at a distance by excluding unwanted sound from the sides of the microphone.

SHOT SHEET   A listing of all shots in the order they are to be made, regardless of their order in the script. It is also known as a shooting list.

SHUTTLE   Movement of videotape back and forth while searching for edit points. It is usually done at speeds faster or slower than real time.

SIGNAL-TO-NOISE RATIO (S/N RATIO)   The mathematical ratio between the noise level in a signal and the program level. The higher the ratio, the better the signal is.

SINGLE-COLUMN FORMAT   A script format derived from the stage script format that is currently used in both feature films and some types of video productions. All instructions and dialogue are arranged down the middle of the page, with various margins and placement of copy indicating instructions, character's names, settings, and dialogue.

SITE SURVEY A detailed listing of all the information needed to shoot on location at a certain site.

SKEW Tension adjustment during videotape playback. It is visible as a "bending" at the extreme top of the picture.

SLANT TRACK Also known as helical recording.

SLATE Several frames identifying the shot, tape reel number, or other logging information. It is usually recorded at the beginning of the tape.

SOCIETY OF MOTION PICTURE AND TELEVISION ENGINEERS (SMPTE) A professional engineering organization that sets visual and aural standards in the United States.

SOFTLIGHT A large light fixture that emits a well-diffused light over a broad area.

SOLARIZATION An in-camera effect created by varying the pedestal and gain to remove portions of the picture or to expand other portions.

SOURCE DECK In a linear editing station, the deck playing back the original footage. Also known as a player.

SPEED The response the camera operator and sound operator give to the director to inform him or her that both of their machines are running at the proper rate before starting to record the shot.

SPLITTER BOX Device used to feed an input signal to more than one output. It is commonly used at news conferences to avoid a jumble of microphones by splitting the feed from one microphone to all those covering the event.

SPOT METER A light meter designed to read a very small area of reflected light.

SPOTLIGHT A lamp designed to provide a hard-edged controllable field of light. Fresnels and ellipsoidals are typical spotlights.

STANDARD DEFINITION (SD) A video signal of lower quality than high definition (HD).

STANDARD OPERATING PROCEDURE (SOP) Predetermined methods of accomplishing tasks. The SOP often is set by corporate or upper management policy.

STANDBY The command a director gives to warn the crew, cast, and others in the studio or on location that a camera is about to roll.

STICKS Another name for a tripod.

STOCK New, unused tape or film before it is exposed to light.

STOP DOWN Decreasing the amount of light passing through a lens. Stopping down increases the f-stop number.

STORYBOARD A series of drawings indicating each shot and accompanying audio in a production.

STRIKE To tear down and pack up equipment and settings from a shooting location.

SUPERIMPOSITIONS (SUPERS) Two or more simultaneously fed video signals, stopping a dissolve at the halfway point.

SWISH PAN A rapid, horizontal movement of the camera while recording. It may be used as a transition device.

SWISH ZOOM A zoom shot accomplished by starting on a scene, and then at the end of the shot, quickly zooming the camera at a high enough rate to blur the image.

SWITCHER 1. In multicamera or postproduction, a device used to change video sources feeding the recording tape deck. 2. The person operating the video switcher.

SYNCHRONOUS (SYNC) Signals locked in proper alignment with each other; sound and picture are locked together, and all the various video signals are in their proper relation to each other.

SYNCHRONOUS PULSES Pulses created either in the camera or in a synchronous generator and added between the fields and between the lines. They are part of the recorded signal, and the receiver locks onto those pulses when the tape is played back or the signal is broadcast. The pulses can be corrected if there are errors in their timing by running the signal through a time base corrector.

TENT An opaque sheet of material suspended over a subject to diffuse and soften the light.

THREE-SHOT A camera composition focused on three people or objects.

TILT The vertical movement of a camera on a pan head.

TIMBRE The perception of a musical note that differentiates the same note from a piano or clarinet.

TIME BASE CORRECTOR (TBC) Electronic device used to lock together signals with dissimilar synchronization. It may also be used to correct for phase, level, and pedestal errors in original recordings.

TIME CODE Time-based address recorded on videotape to allow for precise editing. SMPTE time code is the time code most universally used at present.

TIMELINE The calendar schedule of a production, with each step of the production from beginning to end set as goal dates to be met to keep the production progressing on schedule.

TONE A sound created by generating a single frequency for test purposes and for setting standard levels on recordings.

TRACKING 1. Aligning playback heads on a VCR with the original pattern of video recorded on tape. 2. Movement of a camera to the left

203

or right, usually while mounted on a set of tracks for maximum smoothness and control.

TRANSDUCER Any device used to convert any form of energy to another form: a camera transduces light to video; a microphone transduces sound to electronics; and a speaker transduces electronics to sound.

TRANSFORMER Magnetic, voltage- or impedance-changing device.

TREATMENT A narrative description of a production. It should read more like a novel than a script, because it is intended for people with media and nonmedia backgrounds.

TREBLE High frequencies of the audio band.

TRIPOD Three-legged portable camera support. It is also called sticks.

TRUCK A side-to-side movement of the entire camera mounted on a tripod, dolly, or pedestal mount.

TUNGSTEN LIGHT Relatively efficient, gas-filled light source of approximately 3,200 K.

TWO-SHOT A camera composition focused on two people or objects.

ULTRA-HIGH FREQUENCY (UHF) 1. Frequency band for television broadcasting channels 14 to 69 and some wireless microphones. 2. An older, large, threaded type of video connector.

U-MATIC The ¾-inch videotape format created by Sony in the early 1970s that revolutionized video news gathering. It has been upgraded by a compatible U-matic SP format.

UMBRELLA LIGHT A way of creating a soft, diffused light by focusing a spotlight on the inside of an umbrella designed with a reflective interior surface.

UNBALANCED A circuit usually consisting of a single conductor and a shield.

UNIDIRECTIONAL Microphone pickup pattern from a single direction, coming in a variety of degrees of pickup angle, from cardioid to super unidirectional (shotgun).

UNIVERSAL SERIAL BUS (USB) A bidirectional digital circuit designed to connect a series of digital peripherals with a computer to create an efficient system.

UPLINK Transmission path from an Earth-based station up to a satellite. It is sometimes used to describe the ground station capable of sending a satellite signal. See also *Downlink*.

VARIABLE FOCAL LENGTH LENS (ZOOM) A lens that can have its focal length changed while in use.

VECTOR SCOPE Electronic test equipment designed to show the color aspects of the video signal.

204

VERTICAL INTERVAL TIME CODE (VITC)   Time address recorded within the vertical interval blanking instead of on a separate linear track.

VIDEO   1. Picture portion of an electronic visual system. 2. All-inclusive term for electronic visual reproduction systems; it includes television, cablevision, corporate media, and video recording.

VIDEO HOME SYSTEM (VHS), SEPARATE VIDEO HOME SYSTEM (S-VHS)   JVC-developed consumer videocassette recorder system. The *S* in S-VHS stands for "separate" because it is a semi-compatible component recording system, rather than a composite system.

VIDEOCASSETTE RECORDER (VCR)   A recording system that uses tape contained in closed cassettes.

VIDEOGRAPHER   The proper term for the operator of a video camera.

VIDEOTAPE RECORDER (VTR)   A system that uses tape mounted on open reels.

VIDEOTAPE RECORDER (VTR) SELECTOR SWITCH   Enables a camera to operate with a variety of different recorders made by a different manufacturer than the manufacturer of the camera.

VIDEOTAPE RECORDER (VTR) START SWITCH   A switch that may be mounted on the camera body, but more than likely, it is mounted on the lens handgrip close to the thumb for easy use. This switch allows you to start and stop the recorder without leaving the camera or taking your eye from the viewfinder.

VIDICON   A type of video camera tube that replaced the Image Orthicon; it is lighter, smaller, and more durable, and it provides higher resolution.

VIEWFINDER   The miniature video monitor mounted on the camera so that the operator can see what is framed by the camera.

VISUAL   The video portion of the program.

VOICE-OVER (VO)   Story that uses continuous visuals, accompanied by the voice of an unseen narrator.

VOLT   An electronic measurement of the pressure available at a power source. In North America, the standard is 110 to 120 volts.

VOLUME   The measurable loudness of a sound signal.

VOLUME UNIT (VU)   Measurement of audio level, indicating the average of the sound level, not the peak.

WAIST SHOT   A composition framing a person from just below the waist to the top of the head.

WATT   Measurement of power used in a piece of electrical or electronic equipment.

WAVEFORM MONITOR An electronic measuring tool; both oscillo-scopes and vector scopes are waveform monitors.

WEDGE Plate fastened to the bottom of a camera that allows it to be quickly mounted to a tripod equipped with a matched slot.

WHITE BALANCE Electronic matching of the camera circuits to the color temperature of the light source.

WHITE LEVEL (GAIN) Level of maximum voltage in a video signal.

WIDE SHOT (WS OR LS) The second widest shot in a sequence. A WS is often used as an establishing shot to identify the environ-ment and set the scene.

WILD SOUND Ambient background sound. See also *Nat Sound*.

WINDOW DUB A low-quality copy of original footage with the time code signal visible in the frame.

WIPE Electronic special effects transition that allows one image to be replaced by another with a moving line separating the two pic-tures. Stopping a wipe in mid-movement creates a split screen.

WRATTEN A series of filters originally designed for photography but adapted for use in cinematography and videography.

X-AXIS The plane running horizontally to the camera.

XLR PLUG Professional audio connector that allows for three conduc-tors plus a shielded ground. Special types of multipin XLR plugs are used for headsets and battery power connectors.

Y-AXIS The plane running vertically to the camera.

YOTTA One septillion (1,000,000,000,000,000,000,000,000). One septillion hertz equals a yottahertz (yHz). If yottabytes, measure-ment is useful for indicating digital storage.

Z-AXIS The plane running away or toward the camera.

ZOOM See also *Variable Focal Length Lens*.

ZOOM LENS CONTROL Usually a rocker switch, which allows you to press one end to zoom in and the other end to zoom out. The harder you press, the faster the lens zooms. A very gentle touch produces a slow, smooth zoom. On some cameras, an additional control allows you to set the speed range of the zoom control from very slow to very fast.

ZOOM MODE CONTROL Allows the operator to either zoom the lens manually or use the motorized control of the lens to zoom.

Index